2/19/22

To Marilyn
Thank you for your support. You are Amazing. A pleasure meeting you!

PABLO AGRIO

VetArt USS Iowa

IN PURSUIT OF

HAPPINESS

BookBaby
7905 N. Crescent Blvd.
Pennsauken, NJ 08110
www.BOOKBABY.com

Ordering Information:
For details, contact: agriojulian17@gmail.com
Print ISBN: 978-1-09834-217-3
eBook ISBN: 978-1-09834-218-0

Printed in the United States of America on SFI Certified paper.
First Edition

Disclaimer

This is a work of fiction. Any resemblance to actual events or persons, living or dead, is entirely coincidental.

There is the solitude of suffering, when you go through darkness that is lonely, intense, and terrible. Words become powerless to express your pain; what others hear from your words is so distant and different from what you are actually suffering.

~John O'Donohue,
Anam Cara: A Book of Celtic Wisdom

1

As the year 1975 neared an end, I found myself wondering what was next for me.

I was seventeen and had just graduated from Instituto Nacional high school in my native Panama. I had no real marketable skills, and the unemployment rate was sky high. The Torrijos-Noriega alliance was full of question marks. On the one hand Torrijos was trying to take back control of the Panama Canal from the United States, which promised an economic boost for the country, and on the other Noriega, as his Chief of Military Intelligence, was terrorizing the natives. The future looked bleak. There were rumors of people getting arrested and disappearing, and you had to be careful not to criticize the government in front of spies. I faced two options – either I stayed in school or I found a job and helped my mom with expenses. But before I could decide, my mother informed me I need not worry about that. She'd made arrangements for me to travel to Philadelphia to stay with my godmother and further my "education."

For reasons that were not really clear, my mother made me swear I wouldn't tell anyone about my trip. I guess fear of jealous people sabotaging the trip and good old superstition played a part. I kept my word to the extent that even my girlfriend was kept in the dark about this development, and as a result she suffered a tremendous surprise on the day of my departure. Her tears were genuine, and I felt rotten.

In the moment, I made promises to her that I never kept.

They say that ignorance is bliss, and in this case that proved to be true. I had no idea and couldn't begin to imagine the changes I was about to experience on my arrival to America. A few things stand out in my memory as I try to remember the weeks between graduation in December and departure time. Things such as: getting the travel visa stamped on my passport at the American embassy; sitting in the airplane awaiting take-off and looking out the window at the people I was leaving behind; arriving at Miami International and having to answer questions with my limited English; appearing nervous and anxious and getting sent to an interview room with immigration officials; not knowing where to go for my connecting flight; arriving in Philadelphia and experiencing snow for the very first time. The sight of snow made me feel like I'd landed in Oz.

I guess you could say that things started out okay in Philadelphia. There were lots of introductions, lots of hugs and kisses, lots of "welcome" and "wish you all the best." Everyone was very accommodating. The house, because it was a house, had a strange design. A square box. As you came in through the front door you met the living room, then there was a bedroom, then the kitchen, and at the end, stairs that led to the basement. In the basement there were no room divisions, just beds engaged in social distancing and one bathroom. The furniture didn't match. Someone had made a run to Goodwill or accepted charitable donations. No pictures on the wall. I found out I would be sharing quarters with nothing but women (my godmother's daughters) and two children. I would be sleeping on a sofa bed set up in the kitchen and would be babysitting full time for free.

And the women had priority in using the bathroom. I wanted to ask questions, but truth be told I didn't know where to start.

Days went by, and I hardly left the house. I wasn't shackled nor under orders not to go anywhere. I just didn't have any place to go and was afraid of the unknown. My limited English was a source of embarrassment. Whether it was Monday or Saturday didn't seem to matter much. All my days were the same. I would wake up, tend to the children, wait for the women to return from work, eat, and get ready for bed. One day, during the evening meal, I finally mustered up enough courage to ask when I would be starting with the business of attending college—furthering my "education." The response was slow in coming, but the look of surprise on their faces told me everything I needed to know. They had no idea what I was talking about. And so there I was. I was in the USA but with no clear plan as to my next step in the journey.

One of the girls offered to introduce me to a fellow countryman who was attending high school in the area.

She told me that perhaps he could provide some guidance on what needed to be done. She also asked her boyfriend to drop by and show me around the neighborhood when he had time. Maldo, the high school student, had his own vehicle and delighted in picking me up whenever he had a chance and my schedule permitted. He was about seventeen but acted older. He looked taller than me because of his Afro, and he stuttered when he spoke. There was not an ounce of fat on him. He came from a well-to-do family in Panama and had a happy-go-lucky disposition. I enjoyed hanging out with Maldo because he spoke Spanish and my English wasn't very good. Aaron, the boyfriend, also did his part. Aaron took me around the neighborhood and gave me a sense of what it was like to live in Philadelphia. He was tall and light-skinned. He had a deep voice, laughed a lot, and the word nigga preceded or ended everything he said.

Communicating with Aaron was a bit of a challenge, but he was a good sport about it. He was an Army vet, and his favorite thing to do was smoke marijuana and drink beer. And he didn't mind treating me and sharing his stash with me. Being high provided relief from my daily routine and added color to the snowy streets of Philadelphia. I soon found out that snow doesn't stay white forever.

While doing my babysitting thing, I started to wonder what was next for me. The situation I was in didn't offer any future. Slowly I came to the realization that no one was going to offer direction or suggestions. I had no income, and the roof over my head and the food I ate were being paid by taking care of the girls' kids.

One day, Maldo offered to treat me to fried chicken at the local Geno's Restaurant. While placing the order, we both noticed a Help Wanted sign. We sat down to eat and debated whether I should fill out an application for the position. Eventually we decided there was nothing to lose—so I did. Before leaving, the manager came out and asked me if I had time to do an interview right away. I was hesitant, but Maldo was excited and cheering me on. I agreed and left the interview with a starting date. I wasn't sure how my godmother and the girls would take the news. They were saving a lot of money with me babysitting. But my fears turned out to be unfounded, since they took to the idea without any resistance.

I started out as a janitor but was quickly promoted to cook. There was a lot of overtime available. It was hard work. Employees were constantly quitting or absent. Those present often had to do more than their own assignment. I had nothing better to do, so I hung out as much as possible. As a result, at the end of my day I was exhausted.

I thought a paycheck would ease my pain and discomfort, but I was sadly mistaken. I didn't know it, but my godmother had designs on how that money should be spent. She was a short woman, probably over fifty, that carried over three hundred and fifty pounds on her frame. Her hair was straight, but I couldn't tell if that was natural or because it was processed. And there was a permanent sheen on her face, like perspiration. Something intimidating about her; when she spoke, you listened. Her daughters were all different. The one that introduced me to Maldo was light-skinned and slim, but the other two were definitely big-boned women and wide.

When she broke the news to me, I was disconcerted: on payday, I was to sign my check over to my godmother who would then take money out for my room and board, send money to my mom in Panama, give me $20 spending money, and put the rest in a savings account. I don't really know how much money was sent to Panama or what went into savings. But I knew that this arrangement couldn't last and considered quitting my job.

Right about that time, my mom showed up on a visit from Panama. She and a gentleman friend made a trip to Florida on vacation and while there decided to travel north to visit me. Mom was understandably happy to be in Philadelphia and play catch-up with my godmother. However, at the first opportunity I expressed to her my desire to return to Panama and continue my education there. Of course, she thought that was a ridiculous idea. But I insisted. So when it was time for her to leave, I packed my bags and prepared to return home.

We travelled south on the Interstate via private vehicle, destination Miami, Florida. I enjoyed sightseeing very much and the opportunity to see more of America. My mom and her friend spent the trip trying to convince me I was making a mistake and should return to Philadelphia and make the best of it. I told her I couldn't return to my godmother's home and shared with her what I'd experienced. She then seized on that opening to arrange for me to go stay with Maldo's grandmother. I had a couple of days to enjoy Miami, and then back to Philadelphia via airplane. The highlight of my stay in Miami was a visit to Calder Racetrack to watch the horses run. Then on the day my mom boarded the plane back to Panama, I headed in the opposite direction back to Philadelphia.

Sharing a home with Maldo and his grandmother felt like heaven. I had literally no responsibilities and all my needs were taken care of. Life was so beautiful I didn't give a thought as to what might happen next. After the experience at my godmother's place, I was simply on cruise control. Sleeping late, eating and hanging out with my pals. My English was coming along. Life was good.

A couple of months down the line, I came home one night to find Maldo and his grandmother waiting for me. They said they wanted to talk to me about the future. Right away I felt very uneasy. The look on their faces was ominous. I sat down and indicated I was ready to listen. Grandma went straight to the point: she said that while she loved me like a son, the truth was I couldn't stay with her indefinitely. She said nothing about room and board but mentioned the fact that I didn't have an income and wasn't contributing to expenses. She gave me thirty days to find another place to go, period. There would be no extensions of time and not even a job could save me. Basically, I was being evicted and it was no concern of theirs what happened to me after. I guess they'd given me plenty of time to come up with a plan and I'd failed to realize how delicate my situation really was.

After I received my eviction notice, I became emotionally distraught. There I was, all of seventeen years of age, in a foreign country, with very little command of the native language, about to be thrown out on the streets, no concrete plan for the next day let alone my future life. The sensible thing to do would've been to try to secure enough money for a plane ticket back home. But I really didn't know who to ask for help. Maldo and his grandmother had put up walls when dealing with me. It seemed like they were just counting down the days for me to go. To their credit, they never stopped feeding me.

I wracked my brains trying to figure out what to do. That's when it occurred to me to call a "cousin" I had in Brooklyn. She was the daughter of our neighbor in Panama—not really a blood cousin.

I found her number in my meager belongings and called, not sure if the number was good. To my surprise, she answered. After the initial pleasantries, I quickly explained to her my current situation and asked if I could go stay with her for a little while. She said, "Sure, take the Greyhound bus and I will meet you at 42nd street bus depot in Manhattan."

That evening I broke the news to Maldo and company. They seemed relieved that I'd come up with a plan and wished me luck in my travel. They didn't say I could come back if things didn't work out or call if I ran into any problems, so I knew my departure meant that that bridge had been burned.

I took the bus to New York and settled in for the ride. I kept my eyes on the countryside and fought off feelings of anxiety. I had no money, no plans, and no idea what situation I was heading into. At times I wondered: *What if she doesn't show and I'm left stranded at the bus terminal?*

It wasn't a long trip, right around two hours. When we arrived, I got off the bus and slowly looked around. It seemed like everyone had somebody waiting for them except me. My cousin wasn't there, and I feared the worst. I didn't want to leave the area, afraid that if she showed up late and didn't see me, she would just leave. But with each passing minute the idea that I needed to find a phone and call grew stronger. I sat at one of the benches with my head down and tried to stay calm. I was terrified. My mouth was dry and stomach full of butterflies.

I looked at people, and people looked at me. I don't know what they saw when they looked at me, but I was just trying to find a face that I recognized. I was about to start walking when I saw my cousin running towards me. There was a man with her and two children. She gave me a hug and apologized for being late. She made the introductions and went on to explain why they were late. She was a dark-skinned woman of average height and thin as a twig. I don't think she weighed more than ninety pounds and she had a serious overbite. Her nails were immaculate, and she was dressed like a professional just off work. As she spoke she used her index finger like a maestro uses a baton.

Truth be told I wasn't listening. I just felt such a sense of relief. I was safe again for the time being. One hurdle had been crossed. She had lots of questions about my intentions, and I tried to appear confident. It turned out the fellow that arrived with her was also some "cousin" who was staying with her. So now it was two of us and I would be sharing quarters with him. Her apartment was on the fourth floor of an ordinary-looking building. As you entered the building the first thing you noticed were vandalized mailboxes. The apartment itself was big, but there was so much furniture it was hard to get around. Pictures everywhere, both prints and personal. It was easy to tell no one spent much time cleaning or organizing. The room where I would sleep resembled a closet where people just stuffed things they had no use for anymore.

2

I'd left Panama in January of 1976. I arrived in Brooklyn in April of that year.

After the initial honeymoon period, I quickly found myself in a similar situation to the one in Philadelphia. I was eating food and taking space but not contributing a penny. Soon the questions began about my intentions. My roommate was unhappy with me encroaching on his space and I suspect was talking bad about me to my "cousin." The rumbling got to my cousin's husband who decided I should get up in the mornings and go with him to "hustle." His name was Freddy.

Freddy and I became good friends very fast. He really didn't have a regular job but hung out at a grocery store run by Puerto Ricans in Queens. We unloaded trucks, ran errands, covered for others during breaks, and ran a numbers business on the side. Freddy drank a lot and had a lot of girlfriends. He treated me well and put money in my pocket. His girlfriends liked me and took care of me also. He was a middle-aged man with a noticeable beer belly. He had a tooth gap and smiled a lot. His friendly disposition made him likable. He was always high-fiving people and cracking jokes. According to him, every problem had a solution. You just had to *think*.

All Freddy asked of me was that I keep his confidence. He didn't really know the true relationship I had with his wife but trusted I wouldn't tell on him. Most days we made it back to Brooklyn, but some days we spent the night with one of his girlfriends.

Whenever we made it back to Brooklyn, he'd make a big production of unloading stacks of dollar bills on the kitchen table to keep his wife from starting a scene. I would put a little something on the table also to keep my spot in the apartment. But I could tell my cousin wasn't happy with the situation.

Not much time had elapsed, perhaps a couple of months. One day Freddy left the apartment without me. I stayed put all day, not knowing what to do with myself. I still didn't have answers to the big questions: What was I doing in New York? Where was I heading?

When my cousin came home, I tried to be friendly with her, but she was having none of it. I felt afraid. I knew something was brewing. Soon my roommate arrived and gave me an unfriendly look. My cousin began asking me about things her husband did when we were together. I gave her the politically correct answers, but she wasn't buying any of it. She was angry and exasperated. I tried to stay calm. Then she dropped the bomb on me: since I couldn't be honest with her, I had to leave. Not tomorrow, not the following day, but right away. I was stunned. It was springtime but still a little cold outside. I looked at my roommate, but no help was forthcoming from him. These were my fellow countrymen who knew how dire my situation was, but they showed no mercy, no compassion, no pity or care. Get out and don't come back was their stand. They had fire in their eyes. I went to the room and began collecting my stuff.

I heard the front door open, and it was Freddy. I felt a ray of hope. I don't think my cousin anticipated her husband coming home before my departure. A confrontation ensued between them about my eviction. For all the negatives my cousin pointed out about me, her husband replied that the same could apply to my roommate. The bottom line was she was pissed at me for not telling on her husband and he was wise enough to figure that out. However, as the argument escalated it became clear that he wouldn't be able to save me. He made a phone call, and then told me to get my stuff together and follow him.

He took me to the apartment of a gay Panamanian he knew and asked the fellow to take me in. His name was Ray, and he seemed a decent man. He explained my situation and told Ray that it was a temporary solution until he could figure something else out. I didn't like the set-up, but I simply couldn't think of a better solution on my own.

Just when I thought things couldn't get any worse for me, they did.

Ray drank a lot and most of his visitors also drank and did other drugs. Of course, everyone was curious about me and what I was doing in his place. Who knows what Ray said to them behind my back, but needless to say my reputation took a hit. It wasn't long before I started leaving the apartment early and just wandered the streets until late at night. I figured the less time I spent at the apartment the better off I'd be. A big problem remained—my inability to find employment, and therefore no income. I started meeting people on the streets who were into all sorts of things. *Everyone* referred to themselves as "hustling." I sought out fellow Panamanians in the hope that hanging out with them would prove safer. Maybe I was delusional, but here I am telling the story.

Things that run through my mind as I type these lines, such as never knowing where or when the next meal would come from. When I was evicted by my cousin, it was still cold outside. My coat was good enough to take me from point A to point B but not for hanging out on the streets all day. Clothing was minimal and personal hygiene poor. I drank and smoked dope more than I ate decent meals. I had no plan for the future and no real marketable skills. Anyone who came along and said *Let's go!*—I was game. The interesting thing about all this was that the people I hung out with all seemed to be suffering from the same illness. Someone I came across in this desperate situation asked me if I wanted to earn some easy money. I said sure, I could use some money. He gave me a bag of joints and told me to visit night clubs in the area and offer the joints for a dollar. I would get a cut of whatever I sold. He gave me no other instructions. I was so stupid and naïve I literally walked into clubs within a three-mile radius of Nostrand Avenue and Eastern Parkway in Brooklyn and offered joints to party people without caring if they were narcs.

One night, more like early hours of the morning, I walked into a club on Franklin Avenue and surveyed the scene. Not very many people in the place. I can't remember if it was early Sunday morning or early Monday morning. Days and nights, weekdays or weekends, the exact hour, these things didn't really matter to me. Selling my product was the only priority.

I saw a fellow sitting at the bar sipping a drink and decided to try my luck with him. I sat next to him and asked if he wanted to get high. I told him I had joints for a dollar. He said he was okay. I turned to face the dance floor and see who else I could approach. The guy, who later introduced himself to me as Marty, asked where I was from. I told him I was from Panama. He then said to me, "You came all the way from Panama to settle for peddling joints to strangers? You don't even know if I'm a cop! You keep going like this and you're going to end up in jail or worse." I didn't answer. He kept going, "How old are you? What did you come here to do?"

I said, "To better my life." He started laughing and shaking his head. I became annoyed, got up, and said, "Later."

Marty asked me to wait. He said, "Don't get mad. Here, let me buy you a drink. My name is Marty. What do you want?" I ordered a beer.

Marty then went on to tell me that he was a Marine Corps recruiter and wanted to know: Had I considered going into the service to earn a living? I answered not really. Marty then urged me to think about it. He made me a proposition.

"Let me give you my card. Come down to the station and we'll talk about it. I'll make it worth your while. I'll find something for you to do and put a few bucks in your pocket. That beats what you're doing now, and it's a lot safer. Here are a couple of tokens for the subway. I'll have more for you if you show up."

I made no promises. I finished my beer and walked off into the night looking for clients who wanted to get high. No sooner had I left Marty than I completely forgot about our conversation. My focus remained on the moment. I just couldn't think too far ahead. I checked my inventory and discovered that I'd not sold much that night. That wasn't good. If I sold a hundred joints, I'd get twenty-five dollars. So basically, I was getting 25% of what I sold. Any way you look at it, this was bad business. When I think back on those days, I find it hard to comprehend why I didn't just trying to find a job like a regular Joe. Maybe it was easier to spend time on the streets since I didn't really have a home of my own. Days later, maybe even more than a week, I found the subway tokens in my coat pocket. My first thought was to try to sell them and use the money to get something to eat. Then I remembered my conversation with Marty and found his business card. I knew the address and stood for a moment thinking what I should do. I decided to take the train and go see Marty.

Marty looked like a different man in his Marine Corps uniform. Right away I was very impressed. He seemed happy to see me. He offered me a cup of coffee, and we sat down to talk. He said I could clean the office for him and earn a few dollars. Then I could study for the ASVAB test in preparation for joining the Marines. I hadn't thought about doing this, but like many things in my life up to that point I was making decisions on the go. I don't think I *ever* expressed to him a desire to join the corps. He just kept talking and I kept rolling with it.

And so it was that I began a new routine. Rather than getting up in the mornings and walking the streets aimlessly I now had a place to go and something to do. I kept things to myself as I wasn't sure this was going to work out. But it did. On the day of my 18th birthday, I formally enlisted in the United States Marine Corps. I would leave for boot camp on the first week of January 1977. The question now became how to survive the ensuing weeks and months until departure time. Spring and summer didn't offer much of a challenge. But the winter months would certainly be a problem.

I don't think I weighed more than 115 lbs. I wasn't eating well and certainly not exercising. I told Ray about my plans and asked him to bear with me for a little while longer. He seemed relieved that I'd come up with a plan that had a future. He told me to stop drinking and smoking pot. I heard him but didn't pay any attention. My days remained the same. I would later suffer for that during training. When people heard about my enlistment, their reaction was "you won't make it." I really didn't know anything about the history of the Marines or what their boot camp was like. In retrospect that was a blessing in disguise. Had I known what I was getting myself into I might have backed off.

The remaining months between August and December 1976 were a struggle. The days were long, and the nights short. My immediate social circle remained the same, but now I was more concerned with staying out of trouble. Marty kept reminding me not to screw things up. Money was tight. I was always on the lookout for something that would put money in my pocket. As the weather started to change, it became increasingly challenging to find a warm place to hang out and pass the time. Any excuse to visit someone would do. My situation wasn't unique. A few acquaintances of mine were living day by day in difficult situations. Some of them were in the country illegally. They'd made it this far, but I had no idea what they intended to do going forward. Survival seemed like the top priority. But we took comfort hanging out with each other.

As for me, January couldn't come fast enough. The warm months on the East Coast don't last very long. I'd arrived in Philadelphia in the middle of winter, and this was my first taste of summer in America. There is a different atmosphere all together. People seemed more upbeat, and there was always something going on somewhere. You had parades and fun times at the beach. And at that time, drinking and smoking weed was ordinary stuff. Perhaps it's still like that, but I wouldn't really know.

I tried to take things in stride and just roll with the punches. I was counting down the days for my departure to boot camp, and I thought about that often to keep from becoming gloomy. Ray was still offering shelter, but being around him and his gay friends was tough. While they seemed to respect my choice to stay clear on their deeds, they were always taking shots at me, especially when drunk. Ray enjoyed asking me to run errands with him, and then acted like we had something going on whenever he came across someone he knew. This bothered me a lot because not only was this not true but it damaged my reputation and changed the way people dealt with me afterwards.

I was caught between a rock and a hard place. If I refused to help with the errands, it appeared as if I were incapable of doing the bare minimum to show gratitude for the assistance he was providing. If I turned down invitations, then I was being antisocial and ashamed of his friends. In trying to do the right thing, I accepted an invitation to go to "church" with him. This turned out to be an all-gay event more resembling a "Santeria" gathering than the ordinary Mass I was used to. Lots of singing, chanting, and people being overcome by the "spirit." I wasn't sure what "spirit" and didn't feel the need to ask. Everyone wanted to know who was the new guy, and Ray couldn't help himself. This was nothing physically crippling, but it was emotionally disturbing. I was only 18 and still not capable of sorting through complicated emotions. I decided not to return to that place but would still have to deal with most of the people gathered there for the time I had left. It'd been a long time since I'd visited a barber shop. My hair was long but not straight. It grew more like Garfunkel's fro (from Simon and Garfunkel) or Gabe Kaplan on *Welcome Back, Kotter*.

Today I'm bald and remember those days with a great deal of nostalgia.

I wish I'd done more during my time in New York. I went by Yankee Stadium but couldn't afford a ticket to the game. I walked by the Twin Towers and Empire State Building. I visited Fifth Avenue and Broadway. Just to say I was there. And of course, Central Park. Because I rode the train daily, 42nd Street was a common destination. There was so much more to the Big Apple. But for me it was just a quick introduction and then on to the next twist in my destiny.

3

Christmas and New Year 1976 came and went.

I don't remember anything remarkable happening. My thoughts were on my trip to Parris Island. About a dozen other recruits were traveling with me. I was given the paperwork for all and asked to deliver it to whomever picked us up at our destination. The plane departed from JFK. It was bitter cold. Everyone was quiet, lost in their own thoughts. The trip didn't take long. We arrived in the early morning to find out there was no one at the airport waiting for us. No one knew exactly what to do. Guys began to get restless. Then one of the fellows came and asked me if I thought we should try to make our way to the base. Others chimed in. I realized then since I had the paperwork, I needed to decide. I thought about it, and after looking over the paperwork I told everyone the instructions were for us to wait where we were. Someone would come by to get us and deliver us to the base.

Sure enough, at about five in the morning a bus finally pulled up and a couple of Marines stepped out. They asked for the paperwork, and I gave it to them. They had a roll call, and then told us to get on the bus. We hadn't slept all night, and it would be a while before we saw anything resembling a bed. When we got to Parris Island, the party started in earnest. Right away the screaming began as we were told to get off the bus and line up on the yellow feet painted on the ground. What happened after that remains a blur.

One thing I remember clearly to this day is the visit to the barber shop. I had travelled with what can best be described as a Jewish afro and was proud of it. When I sat on the barber's chair, the guy asked me how I wanted my hair cut. I told him to just tighten it up for me. Not to cut too much. And then without warning he ran the machine right down the middle of my head to my great surprise. I became irate and began to get out of the chair when the drill instructor got in my face and let me have it. I hadn't been paying attention. Everyone was getting their heads shaved. No exceptions. Boy, that was crazy.

After that you go to supply to get your issue. Everything goes in a duffel bag. You eat, get tested, and sign a lot of papers. You become a GI (Government Issue). Well, almost. You still must survive the next three months. This was just day one. My brain was hurting trying to remember the strange new language of the Marines. (Chow for meal time, cover for headgear, skivvies for underwear, trousers for pants, head for the bathroom, squad bay for barracks, et cetera.)

Marine Corps Basic Training is divided into three phases. The first phase is the hardest because there's a lot to learn and get used to and your body is not ready for the physical training it will experience. If you survive the first phase, the second phase is the best. You start to get that Marine Corps spirit and start to look like a unit that can accomplish something. By the third phase all you're thinking about is graduation.

Things that stand out in my memory bank are things like the first physical training test. I did poorly. I was horrible in pull-ups, didn't do well with sit-ups, and the run almost killed me. I think I managed to do two pull-ups. The DIs were on to me. My English was bad, and physically it didn't look like I'd hold up. They determined they were either going to make me or break me. They would have me drop and give them twenty (twenty push-ups) just because. While I was doing the push-ups my anger meter would be off the charts. They'd get in my face and ask what I was doing there and wouldn't it be better for me if I just quit and went back to where I came from.

But quitting wasn't an option for me.

One morning after reveille I was the last one to get in line. I had a little bit of trouble making my bunk. When I got in line, the DI thanked me for finally making it. He then accused me of holding up progress and had everyone drop for push-ups. While we were doing the push-ups, he had everyone thank me for the early morning push-ups. Boy, I was pissed. And keep in mind we hadn't made it to the head (bathroom) yet. So, our bladders were full. I wasn't a popular recruit that day.

Reveille was done by banging on trash cans and hitting the bunks with a baton. And a whole lot of screaming and yelling. Whatever generated the most noise and created confusion. My favorite saying was "drop your cock and grab your sock." I still chuckle when I remember those crazy days.

Other crazy things I remember: getting used to eating fast and running in your boots. And of course, close order drill. You couldn't go anywhere unless you were drilling. And a "blanket party" done on another recruit. Never learned the reason. Don't know if it was a racist attack or poor performance. All I know is that shortly after that I never saw that recruit again.

We started out with about eighty recruits in our platoon. Only about thirty-five graduated. Every week recruits would leave the platoon for one thing or the other. Just when you thought things were settling down, something else would happen. One recruit who was apparently doing well almost drowned during the Swim Qual. In my days you were required to jump off a diving platform in full uniform and remain in the water for a full hour without touching the sides of the pool. I remember him saying he was done but the DIs kept telling him he was close to qualifying so he should hang in there. Next thing you know he was going under. Scary, very scary.

Another scary moment for me was the "slide for life." You're required to start with your chest on the rope, facing the water, and go about a third of the way down before flipping over. I lost my balance right at the start and flipped over. The DI kept screaming at me to get back on top of the rope. I kept trying but couldn't do it. My arms became weak. I wanted to keep going just the way I was but was told if I did, I'd fail the course. Finally, I couldn't hold on anymore and I just let go. I fell into the pool of water. Talk about being scared. Wow! I thought for sure I was a goner. And guess what? Just as they pulled me out of the water, I was told to get back in line for another try. That was probably the lowest point of my boot camp experience. The fear factor was off the charts.

I didn't particularly care for parades either. You always got ready very early, and then had to stand long hours before anything would happen. In the meantime, to go urinate was a huge problem. One parade I sure didn't mind was the graduation parade. I've never felt more elated in my life. I'd made it. Despite the odds, I'd survived. And the physical change was noticeable. I'd put on some pounds and was in tip-top shape. I found out I was to become an artillery man and my next destination was Fort Sill, Oklahoma.

After graduation I had a choice between going back to Panama and asking my high school sweetheart to marry me or returning to New York to do I don't know what. I chose to go back to New York to blow the pocket full of money I had. Bad choice. One of several bad choices and regrets I've had that ended up taking me to the road of perdition.

I guess what it all came down to: I just wanted to show all the naysayers that they were wrong. And you know what? No one cared. The drama was playing out only in my head. The people I had met while in New York (and those in Philadelphia for that matter) didn't care if I was alive or dead. They didn't spend one second of the day thinking about me. That realization bummed me out and made me wish I'd gone back to Panama instead. But it was too late. The dice had been rolled, and all that was left to do was to keep pushing forward.

The one thing I was able to do now that I had money was visit Belmont Park to watch the horses run around the track. I placed a few bets but didn't go completely crazy. I felt alone as I didn't really have any true friends. I was surrounded by a bunch of misfits—drunks, drug addicts, offenders, schemers, liars, manipulators, and the like. I had to constantly be on my toes. Watching and listening carefully. When I finally got on the plane to Fort Sill, I felt a sense of relief, and somewhere in the back of my mind I knew I'd never return to the Big Apple.

4

I loved putting on my Marine Corps uniform.

There's no question that of all the military branches, Marines are the best dressed. Walking through airports and watching people's reaction was something else. I made sure I practiced all that I was taught in boot camp while in public places. I constantly checked myself out to make sure my uniform was correct. I watched what I said, how I said it, and what I did. I didn't want anyone to have anything negative to say about the way I carried myself while in uniform.

Fort Sill is an Army base. It's known as Home of the Artillery. The Marines are a small detachment. It's like we had a little piece of terrain within this huge base. Consequently, it made us Marines stick together like glue—against the Army. Within our own community I got my first exposure to racism. Whites hung out with Whites, Blacks hung out with Blacks, Mexicans with Mexicans, and the rest of us? Well, we just tried to fit in. I met a fellow from Puerto Rico and hung out with him from time to time. I called him Rico.

What I remember most about Fort Sill is that after work there wasn't much to do. We'd go across the street to shoot pool and drink beer just about every day. I began smoking cigarettes because Rico was always offering me one.

First thing they told me when I checked in was to avoid going into town. Since I didn't have a car and there was no nearby public transportation, I didn't think that'd be a problem. However, one weekend, bored out of our minds, Rico got the crazy idea that we should venture into town to check out the nightlife. So, we took a cab to downtown Lawton. Went into a bar with nothing but White patrons in it. We ordered beers and set up the pool table. Everyone was looking at us, but we paid them no mind. There were a couple women sitting at the bar nursing drinks.

After we had a couple of beers, Rico went over and spoke to the women at the bar. He came back and told me we had a date. I was blown away by the news and excited. We met the women at the back of the bar. Rico walked off with one, and the other came up to me and whispered it would be $30. I asked her, "Thirty dollars for what?"

She said, "The date."

Rico had disappeared so I had to decide.

I heard myself saying, "Okay."

When we got to the room, I gave her the $30. She sat on the edge of the bed and prepared to give me a hand job. I stopped her and asked what she thought she was doing. I told her I was paying her $30 for some pussy, not a hand job. She said pussy was more. I asked her how much more. When she told me, I went nuts and told her, "Fuck no. I paid you for pussy, and I'm going to get pussy."

I was a little drunk and maybe a little loud. Next thing I know, a huge biker type White guy came into the room and asked, "Is there a problem here?"

I said, "Who the fuck is you? Get the fuck out of here. This is none of your business."

"Hulk Hogan" spun me around and held my hands behind my back. He told the woman to get all my money, which she did. She got my wallet and took all the money out of it, and then slid the wallet back into my back pocket. He then dragged me to the front door and threw me out. I fell on the ground awkwardly and heard him say, "Get the fuck outta here and don't come back, you fucking jarhead." As I was getting up, another huge White guy was kicking Rico out the door.

We were both pissed and trying to decide what to do. I told Rico the woman had taken all my money. I suggested we call the cops. Rico didn't think that was a good idea. I asked him if he had enough money for a cab back to base. Turned out they took his money too.

We started walking back to base, neither one of us saying much. We came into town looking for an adventure and we found one, all right. No guns and no knives, but the bottom line was that we'd been robbed.

The walk back to base was a long one. We agreed not to tell anyone. I lay in my bunk that morning and thought about what had happened. I was angry and thought about ways to get even. I didn't think it would be hard to find those people again. I just wasn't sure how far I wanted to push the envelope and whether it was a good idea to start down that path considering I was in unfamiliar territory. Needless to say, my pride and ego were bruised and I felt like a chump.

As the new work week began, the bad taste left in my mouth began to disappear. I determined to take it as a lesson learned and to be more careful with where I venture off to in the future.

There was an oddball White guy named Billy who'd bought himself a brand-new Buick Regal. We sort of became friends, and through him I got to see more of Lawton and Fort Sill than I ever would've on my own. I enjoyed hanging out with Billy because he was that rare individual that was just a good, decent fellow with no hidden agenda. He got teased a lot and guys were always messing with him, but he didn't seem to mind. He stayed true to himself always.

As graduation day neared, I was asked to choose my next duty station. I could go east to Camp Lejeune or West to 29 Palms, California. My mom had settled back East and that should've been the deciding factor. But when it came time to put it in writing I chose 29 Palms. All I knew about 29 Palms is that it was near Palm Springs and that this was my chance to see the Golden State. Heck, warm and sunny beat anything the East Coast had to offer.

29 Palms is located in the Mojave Desert in Southern California. It lies on the northern side of the Joshua Tree National Park and includes one of the entrances to the park, at Oasis of Mara. The Marine Corps Air Ground Combat Center 29 Palms is located there. The place probably looks a lot different today than when I arrived in 1977. Back then there was a small community some twenty minutes from base with nothing to offer in the form of excitement. Without a car it was hard to get around. Consequently, the Enlisted Club on base was the default place to unwind. All you could do was drink beer and shoot pool. When Marines got drunk enough, it wasn't unusual to see a fight or two break out.

It was hard to stomach the place, but it was my first duty station and I tried to make the best of it. I made some friends, and while I was there, we managed to visit nearby Palm Springs and even Los Angeles. Come Friday a group of us would get together, rent a car, and take off in search of nightlife. We would take turns driving because there was a lot of highway to cover. Getting into clubs was always an adventure for me because of my age.

I hung out with a Black fellow from Washington DC named Alphonse. He'd been in the Army prior to reenlisting in the Marine Corps. He seemed to know a thing or two. He was in artillery also but eventually worked his way into Public Affairs. He looked like someone who could've played pro football as a running back. He wasn't afraid of confrontation and believed in traveling armed. He was also a racist. He talked bad about White people every chance he had. I'd just listen and not say anything. But it was obvious he had issues when it came to that subject. Whenever we went out together, I always had to be on the lookout for potential trouble and work fast to try to defuse it. Especially if he was drunk. More than once we had to leave a place with Alphonse threatening to shoot someone.

White people were good to me, however. With their help I was able to take care of a couple of things that were extremely important to me at that time.

First, I was standing in formation one morning when the battery's Executive Officer, Lt. Olson—a tall, bespectacled, blue eyed, blond haired man from Wisconsin—introduced himself and gave a rah-rah speech. He seemed the real deal, a guy that said what he meant and meant what he said. He announced that he had an open-door policy and anyone with a problem, personal or otherwise, was welcome to see him during regular office hours. Those words stuck in my head.

I wanted to apply for citizenship but had no clue how to go about doing that. I gave the matter some thought for a few days, and then made up my mind to speak to Lt. Olson about the matter. I went to the office and asked to see him. The clerk wanted to know what about. I told him it was personal. He gave me a look, but I ignored him. Seeing that I had nothing else to say to him he delivered the message. I waited patiently, and after a while the clerk told me I could proceed.

I walked in the office and stood at attention. The Lieutenant told me to relax, sit down, and tell him about my problem. I went straight to the point. I told him I wanted to become a US citizen, that I didn't know if this was something he could help me with but I was coming to him based on what he'd said when he introduced himself to the battery.

Without hesitation he said I'd done the right thing. It was not something he had any personal experience with, but he would research the matter and get back with me. He asked who my immediate supervisor was, and I told him SSgt Willis. He wanted to know if it was okay for him to get SSgt Willis to assist with research. I said it was fine with me.

These two gentlemen went above and beyond the call of duty to help me secure my US citizenship. They helped me fill out the forms and went with me for my interview. We showed up in full uniform and were treated with priority.

The other thing I was able to get done while at 29 Palms was get my first driver's license. Lance Corporal Fitzpatrick, a fellow from Washington State who owned a baby blue 1975 Chevy Monte Carlo, was kind enough to lend a hand with this. Since there was hardly any traffic in the vicinity of the base, he had no concerns with letting me practice in his vehicle. All I had to do was contribute for gas. We did this for a couple of weekends, and then I pronounced myself ready.

He took me to the local DMV for my road test. I was a little nervous and worked hard to appear calm. When I saw the tester, my anxiety grew. He was not the friendly type. Yet, I reminded myself there was no traffic so what could possibly go wrong. We got in the car and he gave me the game plan. Through my peripheral vision I could see him steadily writing on his clipboard. As I took off, I would hear things like, "turn right," "change lanes," et cetera. I didn't think I did that bad, but lo and behold he failed me.

When I walked back to the waiting area, Fitzpatrick asked me what happened. I showed him the paper with all the red markings. I was mad. He told me not to worry. We would practice some more and try again.

A month later we were back for another try. Before we went in, Fitzpatrick said that if I failed again, he was done with me. I would have to find someone else to help me. Talk about pressure. I was all ready for Mr. Hard-ass when instead I get a middle-age white lady with a kind disposition. From the moment we met she was all talk. She asked me if I knew the course and I said I did. Then it was back to friendly conversation. The clipboard stayed in her lap. When I parked, she handed me the paper and told me where to go to have my picture taken. The smile on my face said it all.

These were the highlights of life in 29 Palms. A few months into my tour I'd begun to grow restless. The routine was driving me crazy, and I'd come to the conclusion that desert life was not for me. Outside of drinking and arguing over stupid stuff there was nothing to do. The only women in the area were married or Women Marines (WMs). There were too many of us and not enough of them. I wasn't sure what the solution to the problem was until one morning during formation I heard the Gunny say they needed a volunteer to go to Okinawa, Japan. I didn't think anything of the announcement until I noticed no one was volunteering.

So, just when he was about to volunteer someone, I took a step forward. The time had come for me to leave. The only thing standing in my way was the citizenship thing. With the help of Lt. Olson, I was able to get sworn in and receive my certificate prior to taking leave. It was an amazing thing. I'd come a long ways in a very short period of time.

5

I took some time off before my trip to Okinawa. I was excited about going to Japan. I loved travelling, so I was really looking forward to the trip. Main thing I remember about the journey was how long it took to get there.

Every seat on the plane was occupied. No matter what you did, you couldn't get comfortable. We took off from LAX and stopped in Alaska, then Tokyo. Every time that plane took off it seemed like it wasn't going to get airborne. I'm not afraid of flying, but that was one time I was really nervous about taking off and landing. We didn't get to leave the airport at either stop. We left the plane just long enough to stretch our legs and take a quick look around. If I recall correctly, we fle*w Flying Tigers,* not exactly a household name in American aviation.

When I got to Okinawa I was greeted by nonstop rain. It was unbelievable. I'd just put on a neatly pressed uniform and was on my way to chow when it started pouring. I stood at the door waiting for it to stop so I wouldn't get wet. Another Marine came by and asked what was up. I told him about the rain and he started laughing and said I'd never make it to chow if I kept waiting. He told me to get used to it. It was the season. They had locals who did laundry for you for a weekly fee. I quickly signed up with one. It was the only way to have clean clothes daily.

It didn't take long to get into the routine. There were a lot more things to do and places to go in Okinawa. I was introduced to B.C. Street. B.C. stands for Business Center. All the cab drivers understood that address and that's where the bars and hookers could be found. I became a regular visitor. As time went by and I became more familiar with how things worked, I found a whorehouse I was comfortable with and began to put money aside for my visits which I made on non-payday days. On those weekends the place was almost empty and you got treated a little better. You could take your time and have more fun.

I was spending so much money on cabs that I eventually got my local driver's license and started renting cars at the PX. I also got promoted to Corporal. With my DL in hand and my promotion I was then able to check out Jeeps at the motor pool. I'd get one at lunch and drive to the nearby Air Force base and eat there since the meals were so much better.

It was during one of those trips that I met an Air Force lady that would become my girlfriend. Her name was Ava. She was originally from the Philippines. I first saw her at the Mess hall I frequented and was captivated by her gorgeous smile and beautiful brown eyes. One day, driving back to camp I spotted her on the sidewalk strolling with another airman. On impulse, I turned the Jeep around, pulled up next to her, got out, introduced myself to her, and asked if she'd mind having dinner with me the coming Saturday. She smiled and was about to turn me down when her friend saved the day. Turned out I could see her barracks from where we stood. We exchanged numbers, and the date was set. We both enjoyed dancing and driving around the island. We began to spend all our weekends together.

When we began to sleep together, the subject of birth control never came up. This would prove a serious mistake later. One of the many regrets I have in my life.

Ava and I were separated briefly during the holidays of 1978–1979. My unit was deployed to Korea for training exercises at the DMZ line. I got to experience life on a Navy ship. Getting seasick and dealing with the tightness of space took some adjustment. My respect grew for sailors who do their time under those conditions. It's a heck of a feeling when you stand on the promenade deck and see nothing but ocean all around you, the ship swaying to the rhythm of the waves with tons of cargo on it.

DMZ training was hard work, but it left me with some indelible memories: freezing temperatures and living in tents with gas heaters is no joke. Burning human excrement was one lousy detail. There was a lot of drinking and having sex with "bush bunnies." One of those encounters led me to sick bay for a shot of penicillin.

There was also an incident that left me shook up till this day. A group of us wandered off to the nearby hills to look around. We came across a tunnel. One of the guys said the tunnel went all the way to North Korea. We didn't believe him, so he challenged us to take a look. Me, being young and eager to impress, took the bait.

I started down the tunnel head-first. Not ten feet down things got bad. The tunnel narrowed, and it became pitch dark. I tried to push forward but got stuck. I couldn't go forward or backwards. I started feeling things crawling on my face. I called out for help but couldn't tell if I'd been heard. I panicked and started hyperventilating. I peed on myself and thought I was going to die. I was really scared. Then I felt hands pulling me by my boots. I came out of the tunnel a mess.

The guys were all laughing. I was mad as hell and wanted to fight. I was embarrassed. No one noticed I'd peed on myself because of the amount of clothing we were wearing. I didn't mention what'd happened to anyone for fear of getting in trouble.

I still have nightmares from being stuck in that tunnel.

We were given time off to celebrate Christmas and New Year. We went to Seoul. Of course, this meant more drinking and prostitutes. There was a curfew in place at the time. Wherever you were at midnight, you had to stay there until daylight.

One night I did a mighty foolish thing. We were at a bar drinking beer and watching the girls parade by. I fancied one of the girls and asked her if there was some place we could go. I was drunk and didn't realize it was close to midnight. She nodded, and we left. I didn't tell the fellows what I was doing. I'm not sure where she took me or how we got there. All I know is I woke up next morning with a severe hangover and no idea where I was.

First thing I checked was my wallet.

Thank goodness all my money and papers were still there.

I was so relieved I hurried up and got dressed. I checked and made sure I'd paid her and offered to buy her breakfast, which she gladly accepted. When I ran into my guys again, they were all worried and warned me not to do that again. Even today I shiver at the thought of all that could've gone wrong that night.

All in all, my time in Korea was fantastic. I didn't have a care in the world, and it was all about good times. The same could be said about Okinawa. I felt free and unburdened. I was only responsible for myself. I had no bills to pay and no one to answer to. I did as I pleased. Oh, what a feeling! I wasn't afraid of anything or anyone. The Corps was my family. My guys had my back, no matter what. We were overseas, and it was us against them.

When we returned to Okinawa, I picked up with Ava again. She was my girlfriend, but I really didn't attach any great significance to that. I wasn't emotionally involved. As far as I was concerned, we were just two GIs that got together to have fun with the understanding that sooner or later we'd both be moving to other duty stations. That would essentially end the relationship. It was just an adventure, so much so that I didn't even stop frequenting the whorehouses.

Soon I became a short-timer—that meant my time in Okinawa was up and I was eligible to return to the States. You were obligated to do a year with an option of staying longer if you so desired. I was given my departure date and my next duty station:

The Naval Amphibious Base in Coronado—San Diego.

You'd think the right thing to do was to share this information with Ava. But I didn't. I started avoiding her. When she called the barracks, I'd tell the guys to tell her I was out and to take a message. All her messages said it was urgent that she speak to me.

Finally, I relented and agreed to see her.

When we met, she seemed…distraught? I thought it was because she sensed I was breaking up with her. But it was something completely different. Ava informed me she was pregnant. I was stunned by this news. Didn't know what to say. My first instinct was to ask if she was sure I was the father. Of course, that didn't go over well. Deep down in my heart I knew she wasn't the kind of girl that was out fooling around.

Ava wanted to know what we were going to do. I did my best to pacify her. When we separated, I sat in my room and did some hard thinking. Not about doing the right thing, but about how I could slip into the night unseen and avoid an unpleasant confrontation. I'd decided that her pregnancy was not my problem.

I kept up the charade with her while at the same time counting down the days to my departure. Then I left without saying anything to her. I thought I was in the clear and I'd never hear from her again. I was wrong. I was in Philadelphia visiting my mom when the phone rang. Ava had tracked me down and wanted to know what was up. I screamed at her for locating me, became profane and slammed the phone down, telling her not to contact me anymore. And that was that. Good riddance!

That's what I thought then, but that tape continues to play in my head over and over, especially when I'm having trouble sleeping. I go over how I could've handled things differently. I play the "what if" game. What if I'd just been honest with her and told her I was scheduled to rotate back to the States? We could've exchanged numbers, addresses, agreed to stay in touch. I could've offered to help. Be supportive.

Of course, she may have reacted negatively to all that. She may have argued instead for me to extend my stay, that she needed me there. The question of marriage might have been brought up.

Truth is, I didn't have the tools or the maturity to handle the situation properly. I wasn't ready for commitment or responsibility. I never spoke to anyone about these kinds of situations and just wanted to keep living life care-free and on my terms, unburdened. It didn't occur to me that the decision I was making would find a way to torment long after the affected party would cease to think or even care if I lived or died.

6

It's really amazing how after I hung up the phone with Ava, I deleted the whole episode from my conscious thought.

I'm writing about it, so obviously the memory remained. I hurt more today than I did when it actually happened. What hurts most is the realization that this is one item in a long list of wrongs I've committed that I cannot make whole. I don't know if Ava had the baby or not. I thought I found her on social media and tried to reconnect but received no reply.

I was on leave in Philadelphia, and leave was about good times. I socialized and chased women. I had nothing else in mind. My mom complained that I came home to visit but was never home. I reacted to the criticism with angry outbursts. Another thing I regret is that I didn't notice my brothers had become substance abusers. Rather than helping the situation, I made it worse by actually springing for drugs and alcohol. As far as I was concerned, we were just having a good time.

Since Panama, we really hadn't spent much time together, my brothers and I. In fact, I dare say this was the first and last time we'd all be together under the same roof. The future was dark for all of us, but we just didn't know it then. Mom was right to complain about my behavior. Maybe she had a premonition that her family was about to fall apart but was powerless to prevent it. In the meantime, when I was available, we sat and ate together and enjoyed the stereo equipment I'd purchased in Okinawa.

I pretended everything was okay with them. I didn't want to know if they were happy or sad or if they were dealing with any other emotional or psychological issues. They catered to me, and I felt good about that. Whatever was going on with them? They'd figure it out, just like I was doing.

Soon the time came for me to go to San Diego. I was so looking forward to returning to California, this time to a "real" city. When I arrived, I couldn't believe how nice the place was. I was assigned to a room with another Corporal, but he was never there so that was nice. I quickly discovered, however, that a car was a necessity. Without a car, moving around San Diego was a problem.

I met and became friends with Richie, a Marine from Texas. We had similar likes and dislikes, so the friendship blossomed. He became somewhat of a mentor to me. He took me around town and introduced me to his social circle. Richie was a player. He drove a sports car and dressed the part. I also met Sammy, a Navy guy. The three of us would hit the club scene on weekends and compete to see who'd get lucky with the ladies. But mostly it was just me and Richie.

I grew tired of the transportation situation and took the money I'd been saving to buy my mom a house in Philadelphia and bought a car for myself. You cannot imagine the disappointment felt by my mom when she told me she'd found a house she wanted and the money had gone to the car. I dealt with that situation the only way I knew how to deal with high-stress situations at the time. I rationalized and justified:

Mom's upset now, but she'll get over it in time. It's my money anyway; I can always save up some more. There'll be other homes on the market. Besides, a car's a necessity in California, not a luxury...

This decision would come back and haunt me.

In the meantime, I'd met Maribel through hanging out with Richie. She was five feet tall with long hair, brown skin, and was voluptuous. She had the features of an Indian woman and knew how to work that makeup. She was friendly and easy to talk to. She knew I'd just recently arrived in San Diego, that I was living on base, and that didn't have any transpo'. She and her sister Marta were inseparable. Maribel had a car, so she offered to take me around San Diego and Tijuana to all the party spots. I was grateful for that because it gave me something to look forward to after work. We became fast friends and enjoyed teasing each other a lot. It was interesting listening to them talk about people we'd meet, especially other guys.

I spent so much time with them and received so many calls at the building that Richie asked if I was dating one of them. I told him we were just friends. He then said to me that he thought Maribel liked me and that I should pursue that. I laughed and wondered but didn't give it any serious consideration at the time. Eventually, that would change.

The girls took me to their home and introduced me to their family. It was a large Mexican family. I was welcomed by all except their youngest brother. He didn't warm up to me at all. I didn't let that bother me. I tried a couple of times to make conversation with him, but when that failed, I gave up trying and proceeded to ignore him whenever I visited the house.

One day, while visiting them, Maribel asked me to go run an errand with her. Marta was busy so it gave me a rare chance to be with her alone. I decided to follow up on what Richie had brought to my attention. I asked her how comes she didn't have a boyfriend. She said she hadn't met anyone that was boyfriend material. I laughed, and then asked her directly if she liked me. She took her time answering me, and when she did, she said I was okay, but she was afraid that I was just like Richie—a player who couldn't be trusted. She was so right about that but would eventually ignore the evidence and open her heart to me. Poor girl, I was the last guy in the world she wanted to believe in. I saw San Diego as an extension of the life I'd started overseas. I didn't really have any serious plans for the future. I was just drifting, living day by day. Anything that was fun was okay. Anything that brought about responsibilities was not okay. Responsibilities began and ended with my work hours. I believed everyone around me felt the same way. I had no other perspective. And there was just no one to challenge that belief system.

The Marine Corps' birthday is celebrated every year on November 10th. In 1979, on or about that day, the Marines stationed at NAB Coronado held their traditional ball. Richie invited his girlfriend Victoria, and I invited Maribel.

The plan was for us to spend some time at the ball and then move the party to Tijuana. We were dressed in our uniforms with the girls in evening gowns. We all had a different outfit for the trip to Tijuana. It was an evening full of fun and laughter. But the devil was working in me.

Maribel carried herself with a lot of spunk and sass. In talking to her you would've thought she'd been around the block a few times. I believed that, but later I'd find out different. She was hot and sexy, and that night she really looked spectacular.

When the time came for us to leave the ball, I convinced her to go with me to the barracks so I could change. I knew the place would be deserted since everyone was at the ball. And once in my room it was all about making love to her. To my surprise she seemed tense and anxious. I asked her several times if she was feeling well. I thought she was afraid that I could get in trouble for having her there, but it turned out that wasn't the case. After making love I grabbed a towel and was heading for the shower when I noticed blood on my private parts. My first thought was that Maribel was on her period.

I looked at her and asked her to check herself because I had blood on me.

She was slow to respond.

Then it hit me.

I sat on the bed next to her and took her hands. We made eye contact, and I said, "Was this your first time?" She nodded. So, we sat there in silence both of us lost in our own thoughts. Finally, I asked her if she still wanted to go to Tijuana or did she want me to take her home. She chose Tijuana. I took a look around the building to make sure we were still alone and, satisfied that we were, I took her to the shower room so we could clean ourselves up. We then got dressed and left for TJ.

Once at the club in Tijuana we met up with Richie and Victoria. With those two sitting with us the mood improved dramatically. We danced and laughed and had a swell time until almost dawn. I took Maribel home, and her mother insisted I stay with them. She fixed a nice little spot for me to sleep in, and I slept like a baby until right around the noon hour. When I woke up, I was treated to lunch before heading back to the base. Maribel's life had changed—but for me it was just another fun day.

That family couldn't have been better to me. From the very first time I met them, no doubt. But on this day, it was like they were saying *You too are family now*. I would've spared myself all the grief that came upon me later had I been wise enough to appreciate what had been offered to me.

I'd turned 21 in August, so I no longer had to worry about being carded at clubs. Every weekend was a party weekend. My social plate was full. I enjoyed being with Maribel but didn't think of her as my main squeeze. I went out with the boys as often as we could get together and dated other girls. A couple of times I ran into Maribel at clubs in Tijuana while with another date. She never made a scene. She just looked at me long and hard with sad eyes. I'd get so uncomfortable I'd just leave.

Things at work were going well. I was selected to be the Colonel's personal driver. This was a momentous occasion because as our working relationship grew, he got me to start thinking big-picture about my career and encouraged me to work towards becoming an officer. This brought about a shift in my thinking. For the first time as a Marine I now had a particular goal in mind, something to look forward to. I'd been wrestling with the prospect of whether I should re-enlist or not, and this possibility helped in my decision. My four-year contract was up at the end of 1980. But while I was busy putting all this together, up comes Maribel and tells me she is pregnant. This bit of news threatened to change the course of my life, or at least that's how I felt at the time. I spoke to the boys about what was happening and sought their advice. It was unanimously believed that a child would bring on responsibilities that would make it difficult for me to pursue a college degree and a commission as an officer in the Marines. I was torn by what to do. However, I eventually convinced Maribel to have an abortion.

May God forgive me for that and all the other serious errors in judgment I went on to make.

Maribel's mom and the rest of her family gave me an ultimatum—marry her or leave this house and never come back. I got up and walked out of the house with Maribel's loud sobs ringing in my ears. A true scoundrel.

Maribel's life was essentially destroyed. I learned later that she was asked to leave the house right after I'd departed. She survived by staying here and there with friends and eventually became pregnant again by someone else.

I went back to base to continue with the pursuit of my goal. I don't think I spent a whole lot of time thinking about what I'd done. With the

Colonel's recommendation I was accepted to the BOOST program at the nearby Navy base. This was a program designed to give minorities an opportunity to study and improve their SAT scores prior to applying for a college scholarship. I was elated. Everything was going according to plan.

I re-enlisted and was promoted to Sergeant. I moved off base and became roommates with Rosalba, a Puerto Rican lady I'd met at a night club. The BOOST program was a year and a half long. I dedicated myself to it and couldn't imagine not securing a scholarship for myself.

I took my re-enlistment money and bought myself a Mazda-RX7 sports car.

Part of me felt I should've taken that money and make good on my promise to buy my mom a house. But part of me felt I needed to upgrade my ride to go along with the image I'd created for myself. I kept my decisions to myself to avoid disagreements and criticism. The car payments plus insurance severely impacted the amount of spending money at my disposal. I kept telling myself that that was a good thing because staying put meant I could concentrate on my studies.

The year and a half I spent at BOOST was incredibly rewarding. I improved my English vocabulary and my writing skills. I continued to socialize and meet interesting women. Imagine my good fortune when I was assigned Officer of the Day duties at the women's quarters. Yep, life was good. I was one of a handful of students that had a car and an apartment off base. And I was single. The Mazda was paying dividends, and I was never in need of a date. Often, I would find notes from admirers on the car's windshield. My ego was out of control. The only thing that was worrying me was that, despite being at the top of my class, my SAT scores remained low when compared to the competition. I'd taken the test twice and was just above 1200.

In the end, this would prove fatal to my dreams of a scholarship.

Thirty-three Marines were competing for twelve scholarships. When it came time to announce the selectees, we gathered in a conference room for the news. The Captain didn't waste time. The first name he read started with a "C." When I realized he was going in alphabetical order I felt like crying. I'd missed the cut.

I stood in my spot paralyzed with grief. Fighting back tears I could see the selectees congratulating each other. The joy and happiness in their faces was priceless. It occurred to me that I should be wishing them well, but I simply couldn't speak. The Captain then dismissed those of us who were not selected. He told us the program had ended for us and we would be receiving orders to return to the fleet within a couple of days. Word came down that an impromptu gathering was being organized to celebrate with the selectees. But my heart wasn't in it. I was bitterly disappointed.

Up to that point I'd never failed at anything in my life. It was a massive blow to my ego. I didn't stick around to finish the workday. It was like nothing mattered anymore. I drove to my apartment, sat on my bed, and cried like a baby. I didn't know it then, but I went into some kind of deep depression. I couldn't eat, couldn't sleep, and didn't want to talk to anyone. I'd put all my eggs in one basket. There was no Plan B. I dreaded the idea of returning to the fleet. I'd been out of artillery for a long time. It occurred to me that I'd probably end up at Camp Pendleton. My life and lifestyle would change, no doubt. I didn't want to go back to the fleet, but I had no choice. It was inevitable.

I developed a negative attitude that would stay with me for years.

7

Duty at Camp Pendleton meant no more dress uniforms and classroom environment. It was time for combat uniforms and boots.

The second half of 1982 would prove dreadful, and it would only get worse. The Captain in charge of the artillery battery expected a great deal of me. However, I'd not done any artillery work in a long time and was ill-equipped to lead the men in my unit. I found myself under a lot of stress as I tried to catch up. I hated the job and didn't want to be there, so that attitude wasn't helping things. I was sent back to Fort Sill, Oklahoma, for re-training. Bummer.

I came back from Fort Sill feeling no more confident than when I left. I was living on base now, sharing a room with another Sergeant. The man played jazz music 24/7. I told him I had a tough time sleeping with the music on. He said he had a tough time sleeping without the music. He said he'd keep it at a low volume. I thought to myself an apartment was a must.

I was stationed at Camp Las Pulgas. The place reminded me of 29 Palms. It was more than a little depressing. You had to drive to nearby

Oceanside for any civilian activity. I'd lost my social circle and found myself bored to death on weekends. I met and became friends with another Sergeant living a couple of rooms from mine. His name was Larry. He was originally from Miami, Florida. He too wanted to find an apartment and leave the base. So, we worked together to find an apartment to share, as individually we couldn't afford it.

After moving off base, I took some time off and went to Philadelphia to see mom and clear my head. There I met Agatha. She was a welcomed distraction. She took me around Philadelphia and showed me a side of the city I'd not seen before. She was a part-time DJ for a little-known radio station, so she knew people. She had short, curly hair and a dazzling smile. Her eyes were big and brown—staring at them made you dizzy. She carried herself with confidence. We had a good time, and prior to my returning to California, agreed to stay in touch.

Back at work things didn't improve one bit. I was constantly in the doghouse with the Captain. As 1983 began, I found myself struggling to get a sense of direction with my life. Part of me wanted to pursue a scholarship and finish what I started at BOOST. But with the struggles at work, my confidence was low. I was also facing the end of my three-year contract and had to decide whether I'd re-enlist or not. And if not, what would be my next move?

I re-connected with Richie, my old friend from Coronado who was now living in Santa Ana. The drive to his place wasn't a long one and visiting with him allowed me an opportunity to talk about decisions that were coming up and get a different perspective. We also got right back into enjoying the night life. We'd put on our "Sunday best" and just drive around checking out different spots all over Los Angeles and neighboring areas. Partying was like taking a pill to get rid of allergies. Once the medication wore off it was back to dealing with the symptoms.

Like I said, 1983 was a rough one.

First, I re-connected with my old friend Lola (a stocky Mexican woman who looked like she could play football) at a night club in San Diego. She used to be in asset protection at a department store in the valley. She was now a police officer. We hadn't seen each other in a while, so we took our time catching up. I told her about my situation at work and how unhappy I was. She listened, and then told me the police department was looking to hire more minorities and my military background would be a plus. She gave me a number to call and encouraged me to check it out. She said she thought I would do well in policework and it could be an alternative to re-enlistment.

I took her suggestion seriously, and after thinking it over and doing some research, I made the call. I decided that if I was offered the position, I was done with the Corps.

Second, Richie's brother came from Texas to stay with him. I found this out during one of my visits. Richie and I were not much into drinking or doing drugs. But his brother was. Richie and I had a mellow way of hanging out. Not so his brother. The dynamics had changed somehow. His presence alone made things different. There was a lot more discussion about what to do and where to go. Richie seemed to try very hard to please him. When going out we now had to take both cars since Richie also drove a two-seater.

It was on one of those party nights that I'd experience the first serious traumatic event of 1983. We were at a club in Long Beach, partying and drinking. I'd followed Richie and his brother there. Richie picked up a chick and was going to spend the night with her. His brother would ride back to the apartment with me. We were both drunk and shouldn't have been behind the wheel. Prior to leaving the club's parking lot, Richie's brother asked if he could drive us back. I didn't think twice about it and switched spots with him. Big mistake. My boy decided to test the Mazda

RX-7, and while travelling at a high rate of speed he lost control of the vehicle and crashed.

The vehicle was close to being totaled, but more heartbreaking was that he ended up a quadriplegic.

Life for all of us was never to be the same.

His family blamed me for the accident.

Inexplicably, even though neither one of us were wearing seatbelts, nothing happened to me. Not a scratch. At the hospital, I had to make decisions about his medical treatment that should've been made by his family. In the aftermath, I tried my best to reach Richie to tell him what had happened, but I had no idea where he was. I finally got hold of him when he returned to the apartment at daylight.

He was understandably devastated. I went over what happened several times with him. A question he asked made me very uneasy. He wanted to know why I'd allowed him to drive, knowing he was drunk. The friendship was fractured. I stayed supportive for months after the accident but eventually reached a point where I couldn't handle it anymore.

Struggling to deal with the nightmares of the accident, I had the bright idea to invite my friend Agatha from Philadelphia to come spend time with me at my apartment in Vista. Larry had moved out on me, and I was having a tough time finding a reliable roommate. The expenses were mounting. I needed a pleasurable distraction. Agatha's arrival seemed heaven sent. But I was mistaken. The woman that came to California wasn't the same woman I'd met in Philadelphia. It was Agatha alright, but she was different. Our first clash came when she demanded that I leave my car with her so she could get around the city while I was at work. I mean, the Mazda wasn't the same after the accident, but it was still *my* Mazda. I said, "No way, Jose." She was pissed.

I could tell she was plotting and getting ready to strike. I just didn't know how or when. I kept my eye on her. However, I didn't do a good job. She got hold of my credit cards and went on a shopping spree.

Also, a Sergeant that worked with me came by the apartment ostensibly looking for me. I'd made the mistake of telling him about Agatha. They met and kept it from me. I found out one day when I saw her pulling up to the apartment driving his car. She was staying with me but wasn't paying rent, wasn't contributing to food, and had stopped giving me pussy. I felt like the biggest fool to ever walk the face of the earth.

I had no peace of mind, trouble sleeping, and consequently felt tired all the time. I couldn't stop thinking about my situation and kept searching for possible solutions. That's when the next blow landed. My mom called to tell me that my older brother had died in a car accident. Apparently, he and my younger brother had been out drinking. He drove my younger brother home, and on his way home fell asleep at the wheel. He was on a freeway overpass, so the car fell quite a ways before final impact.

I told Agatha what had happened and told her we were going back to Philadelphia. She said, "No, *you're* going to Philadelphia. I'm staying here." I told her if that was the case, I wanted her out of the apartment by the time I came back. She wanted me to leave my car keys with her. Seriously?! When I arrived in Philadelphia, I found my mom devastated. Her son had died a horrible death, and now his wife wanted my mom excluded from all funeral arrangements. I couldn't believe what I was hearing. I quickly got in touch with the wife and arranged for a meeting. After arguing for hours and trading insults, her parents stepped in and told her she needed to recognize my mom's suffering.

Prior to burying him, there was a memorial. It was supposed to be a closed-casket, but I insisted it be open-casket. I wanted to see my brother one last time. The funeral director strongly advised against my request. In the end I had my way, and what I saw shocked me and left me perpetually dazed. Think Frankenstein.

He was buried on my birthday in 1983. I returned to California with my head all screwed up. Agatha had moved out and was staying at a motel with my co-worker, the Sergeant. He thought I was mad at him for "stealing" my woman, but I was secretly pleased that he'd taken her off my hands. Sadly, things didn't end well between them. She left him and returned to Philadelphia but not before leaving him with a pile of bills and crashing his car.

I continued to have problems with the roommate situation. That's when I had another bright idea. I asked my mom if she wanted to come stay with me. She quickly jumped at the opportunity. In theory it seemed like a good plan. But my mom didn't know how to drive, and navigating public transportation would prove a challenge. Things in California were not the same as Philadelphia.

In the meantime, my application to become a police officer was moving forward. All indications were that I would be offered the position. I'd passed the background check, and it was just a matter of putting on the finishing touches. This welcome news freed me from the stresses I was experiencing at work. I gave notice that I wouldn't be re-enlisting and gave up all pretense of caring about my job. The Captain recognized my attitude and quickly took me out of artillery and put me in charge of getting details to the rifle range for qualification. I had to get up real early for this, but it was easy duty. As a Sergeant, I just gave orders and made sure everyone that was supposed to be on the detail was present and accounted for. At the end of the day I made sure all rifles were cleaned and properly secured in the armory. I was usually done by 1300 hours.

The rest of my days were spent getting organized and ready for the transition to policework. I had to find an apartment in San Diego. The drive from Oceanside every day wasn't something I wanted to deal with.

Meanwhile, my mom was proving to be a trooper. She was figuring out how to get around and had secured employment. But her days were long, and she wasn't happy. I don't know what else I could've done to help with the situation. I was very busy myself and had a lot on my mind. So, we just kept pushing forward, hoping for a better tomorrow.

From time to time I'd think about Richie and the situation with his brother. I wondered how things were coming along and felt I should reach out to them. But I was afraid I'd just open the door to more recrimination. I determined to just put those thoughts on hold and concentrate on the new challenges ahead. I did all I could to learn as much as I could about the police academy and what to expect. I was honorably discharged from the Marine Corps on a Friday afternoon and reported to the police academy the following Monday morning.

Yep, no vacation, no breaks. I just went right into it.

8

The police academy proved to be a bit of a challenge.

Looking back, I had a tough time making the transition from Marine Corps Sergeant to just another recruit. I thought my boot camp days were over with. As a result, I had a terrible misunderstanding with a female Hispanic training officer. I took offense to the way she spoke to me during a particular training exercise. I said some things I shouldn't have said, and she filed a complaint against me. My career almost ended before it began. Luckily for me the reviewing officer was a former Marine and he gave me the benefit of the doubt after I issued some serious apologies. However, I was branded and left the academy with a "can't take orders from women" jacket. Not surprisingly then, during my probationary year I'd often find myself working with a woman or for a woman.

Something else that I found difficult to understand at the time was how much trouble I was having firing the service revolver. Granted, I dealt with rifles and .45 caliber pistols as a Marine. Qualifying with an ordinary Smith & Wesson six shooter should've been a breeze. But no matter how hard I tried I couldn't hit the center target! I barely made it out of that test.

I was at the top of the class academically and holding my own physically, but this part of the program had me on the ropes. The answer came to me months later when I was forced to see a doctor behind serious headaches. Turned out I needed eyeglasses. How about that?

After graduating from the academy and surviving the three months of on-the-job training with corresponding daily evaluations, I was assigned to foot patrol in the San Diego downtown area to help eradicate drug dealing, loitering, panhandling, and prostitution.

I was supposed to make contact and document field interviews of potential suspects. I had no idea how you determined who might be a potential suspect. My partners didn't take time to explain anything to me. I was supposed to learn by observing. This approach got me into hot water. I tried to do a field interview with a female I noticed standing around at an identified "hot" corner. She didn't look like a prostitute, but I figured you never knew. She became irate with me and refused to provide identification. I wasn't expecting this response and didn't know what to do. People were looking at the exchange. I felt I couldn't just let her get away with ignoring my request. So I threatened to arrest her. She then complied but was pissed out of this world. She asked for my name and badge number, which I provided. Next thing I knew I was dealing with a Citizen's Complaint.

I just kept stepping into poop every chance I got. And there was always a woman in the middle of it. Once more I came close to not making my probationary period.

My career as a police officer was otherwise unremarkable. I worked hard to get out of patrol as soon as possible. After three years, I did a short stint as a school officer for a while, and then was selected to participate in a pilot program known as DARE (Drug Abuse Resistance Education), which meant taking the "just say no to drugs" message to elementary school kids.

However, just before the one-year probationary period was up and while I was still wet behind the ears, I had to overcome a truly ugly experience. While riding shotgun with a White officer, I was involved in a situation in which my partner and another White officer friend of his became abusive towards a young Black man in the Logan Heights area. I did not know at the time that they were racist individuals who got their kicks from harassing Blacks hanging out at the street corners.

The situation started as a typical Q&A, but when the young man refused to cooperate on the grounds that he hadn't done anything wrong, things got out of control. People started to bunch up around us while hurtling insults of all kinds, so the two senior officers decided to put the fellow in the back seat of one of the patrol cars by any means necessary. The young man fought and resisted with all his might. This in turn caused the officer who had initiated contact to respond with violence. I kept my eyes on the crowd. With the young man secured in the back seat of the patrol car, we left the immediate area in a hurry.

A few blocks away the error in judgment was compounded. The senior officer decided to let the fellow go with a verbal warning. No arrest was executed, and therefore no report was filed. Within minutes of the incident the Sergeant requested a meeting with all of us. Prior to meeting the Sergeant, we met ourselves and came up with a story we were supposed to stick to in order to avoid trouble. We would state that we suspected the guy of being under the influence of PCP, but after a more complete evaluation we concluded he was not and so we let him go. But trouble wouldn't be denied. The situation became political and incendiary in a hurry, and I found myself right smack in the middle of it. The young man suffered various injuries, and community leaders got involved. The White officers pressured me to stick to the contrived story, and the Black officers wanted to know why I was sticking up for them. I held out for as long as I could.

I guess the straw that broke the camel's back was when I was summoned to a meeting with a high-ranking African-American female officer who reminded me that I was on probation and could be terminated at any moment without cause. She also told me that all the facts were in and witness testimony recorded and that that meeting represented my last chance to come clean and save my job. My lawyer asked her what kind of discipline I'd face if I changed my story. She answered that whatever it was it wouldn't be as bad as being fired. He advised me to cooperate. I told the truth. Nothing more, nothing less. My partner was suspended and received a letter of reprimand. I received a letter of reprimand. The other officer was fired.

When the dust settled, the locker room at work became a hostile environment for me. White officers did everything they could to provoke me into a fight. They called me "yellow-belly," "spic," et cetera, and told me not to back them on any calls. Black officers pretended not to notice, as did other Hispanic officers. The situation became even more dangerous when I was out on patrol and my radio transmissions requesting backup or assistance would be stepped on. I notified the White supervisor about this, who then told me I was imagining things. I wasn't invited to socialize with the crew anymore, and working with a partner was a challenge due to lack of communication and poor attitude.

I never forgot this incident, and it changed my opinion about the men and women who worked for the department. It was a culture that was foreign to me. From that point on, I felt alone and didn't trust anyone to have my back. I decided I needed to get my law degree and get the hell out of there as soon as possible. I also knew I had to get out of patrol no matter what or risk losing my life. In that vein I made up my mind that while working alone if I contacted a citizen and they refused to follow my instructions or resisted arrest I would just let it be. I wasn't going to get into a wrestling match with anyone over trivial stuff and then have to bring the use of force into the picture, lethal or otherwise. No one was going to look out for me, and either way I went I was going to end up in a world of hurt, all to my detriment.

Therefore, I volunteered for all the non-exciting details such as burglary reports, guarding crime scenes, towing abandoned vehicles, working traffic accidents, transporting prisoners to jail, and so forth. And when there was no other choice I calmly explained to my contacts, up front, that I was just trying to do my job and a little cooperation would be seriously appreciated. The alternative was for me to leave, and then they'd have to deal with the White cavalry when they came later. I thought I was being slick then, but didn't realize I was voicing an impression of the state of affairs in our country regarding race and law enforcement.

The last thing I want to say about my experience as a police officer is the distinct impression I had of guys looking for opportunities to shoot and kill someone. And by someone I mean a minority. This action brought them instant celebrity status and set them apart from the herd. A spot in SWAT was theirs for the asking not to mention membership in an exclusive club—cops who'd killed, maybe murdered, someone and gotten away with it. Today these memories sadden me, especially given the recent developments in our country.

Law enforcement is a tough job. It requires a multitude of skills. I don't know that there is anyone out there that can say exactly what kind of training should be given to encompass all that is needed. What I do know is that it must include White officers acknowledging their racist and prejudiced attitudes and dealing honestly with their fear of the African-American man and Blacks, on the other hand, tempering the utter hate and contempt they have for anyone carrying a badge of authority. Without that there will be no healing or progress in our communities. However, the history of slavery and racism and the suffering that endures gives me no optimism that change will come in my lifetime. Poverty and crime are staples of our communities, and confrontations will undoubtedly continue. There is no magic pill, and opinions are as diverse as individuals. Rodney King asked the question, "Can we all just get along?" Perhaps the answer to the question can be found in Michael Jackson's song "Man in the Mirror." We should all start with that.

During that time, I often took lunch breaks at a local restaurant, which was part of my beat. The staff there was friendly to police officers and you could find a secluded spot where you could eat without being bothered. Andrea was the manager, and whenever I came in, she'd find time to sit with me and my partner for small talk. She was a beautiful young woman, with a fair complexion and a model's body. She reminded me of the Mexican actress Maria Felix. She was high energy and loved to talk about police work. She seemed very innocent. One such night, after we left the restaurant, my female partner asked if I was dating Andrea. I said no, and then asked her why she thought that.

My partner proceeded to tell me that, based on her observation, it was clear that Andrea liked me and that if I liked her, I should ask her out. I considered the possibility, but with all the bad luck I was having with females since I joined the department I decided to just wait and see. However, I didn't have to wait long. The very next time I dropped by the place to have lunch, Andrea invited me to her sister's birthday party. We talked about it, and she gave the date and instructions on how to get to the hall. I told her I'd arrive a little late since I had to work that day.

When I got to the party, I had a tough time finding parking. Low riders everywhere. I also noticed a lot of young *cholos* hanging around. For a moment I thought I had the wrong place. I was dressed in a conservative suit and carried my off-duty detective special. I felt uneasy about the whole setup. I wondered if the young gangbangers could tell I was a cop and maybe try to start trouble. I decided to check out the place anyway.

When I walked into the hall the mariachi music was going full blast. I looked around for a minute but couldn't see Andrea. I then approached a lady at one of the nearby tables and asked her if she knew where I could find Andrea. She signaled for me to wait, and then instructed one of her tablemates to go find her.

When I saw Andrea, I could tell right away that she was very intoxicated. Her speech was slurred, her eyes red. She greeted me with a hug and a kiss and asked me if I wanted something to drink. I declined. A young man came by and asked her to dance, and she took off with him. I stood there surveying the situation and decided it was time to go. However, I waited a bit so I could tell her of my decision. When she was done with the dance number and returned to where I was standing, I told her I was leaving and thanked her for the invitation. She asked for my telephone number and address, so I gave it to her. I then left the area in a hurry and drove home to get some rest.

I was in a deep sleep when the phone rang. It was Andrea. She said she was at my apartment complex but having a tough time finding my unit. I gave her directions to my place and wondered what was up.

My mom and I had made the move from Oceanside to a nice apartment complex in the valley near Jack Murphy Stadium. It was a two-bedroom place, and the complex featured a gym and swimming pool. It was also hard to find a particular unit if you were not familiar with the layout.

Andrea rang my doorbell, and when I opened the door, she was in no better shape than when I'd left her at the party. She walked into the apartment like she owned the place and went straight to my bedroom. She took her clothes off and jumped in my bed. My mom heard the commotion and asked me what was going on. I told her to go back to sleep as all was well.

Looking back at this situation, there were a number of things I could've done differently and in the process saved myself much grief. I could've called her a taxi and sent her home. I could've told her to put her clothes back on and drove her home myself. I could've let her stay in the bed and simply moved to the couch. Instead, after admiring her figure for a moment I took my pajamas off and joined her in bed.

As daylight broke, she got up and was on the move again. I was amazed at her recuperative powers. I was still in bed unwilling to give up my sleep. I thought she was just using the restroom, but then I heard her say she'd call me later. And that was that.

When I finally got up, my mom wanted to know what went down. I avoided the subject, as I myself was trying to put things in perspective. I wasn't sure if what I'd just experienced was nothing more than a one-night stand or if there was more to follow. I thought about calling Andrea but decided against it as I didn't really know what I'd say. We'd really never had a meaningful conversation with each other. I kept replaying the events of the past day in my head, unable to come to any definite conclusions. I went to work that afternoon and tried not to think any more about what had taken place. At lunch I chose a different place to eat to keep from feeling awkward around her. However, before the end of my shift a co-worker delivered a message that Andrea wanted to see me.

I worked my way to her restaurant, and when she saw me, she came from behind the counter and took me to her office. She told me she'd told her mom that she'd be spending the night at a friend's place but planned on dropping by my place again. She said she was tired of living with her mom and was actually trying to find her own place but at the moment couldn't afford it. I listened and offered no objections to her plans. We made out a little bit, careful that I wouldn't get lipstick all over my face and uniform. I thought about my mom and what I'd say to her. I secretly wished that she'd be asleep when I got home so I wouldn't have to explain anything. But deep down I knew that something needed to be said and soon.

The spending the night at my place quickly became routine. I looked around and Andrea's stuff was all over the place, so I had to make room in my dresser for her. My mom met her and wasn't impressed. She peppered me with questions: "Where'd you meet her? How long have you known her? Where does she live? Who does she live with? Why is she spending so much time here? Is this serious? Aren't you going too fast? Did you meet her parents?..." Et cetera.

The bottom line was that my mom felt I was moving too fast for my own good. Typical of me at that time, I reacted to her concerns by thinking that she was trying to tell me how to live my life. Since I didn't have any good answers to give, I'd respond with angry outbursts. I'd remind her that I was a grown man capable of making my own decisions. Hmmm...

I'd met and become close friends with a fellow named Nick and his father Pedro. Nick had graduated from law school and was studying for the bar exam. Nick loved the club scene, which is how we met. His father was a great cook and a good car salesman. Because of the nature of my job, I had a very limited social circle. Enjoying a good meal with these two was about the only thing I did besides work.

Andrea came up with the bright idea of going dancing. She said if I had a friend, we could make it a double date. I asked Nick if he was interested. I told him about Andrea and what had transpired between us. Like my mom he was full of questions and concerned that I wasn't thinking straight and rushing into things. Nevertheless, he agreed to go on the double date just so he could meet her.

We agreed to meet at a club near San Diego Harbor. Up to that point the only nagging feeling I had was how she was going to get in the club since she wasn't yet twenty-one. Other than that, I expected the evening to be fun. A little dancing, a little socializing, and then home.

I met Nick in the parking lot of the club at the designated time. We looked around but saw no sign of the girls. Nick then suggested we go inside and see if perhaps they were already there.

We walked around slowly looking for any sign of them. I finally spotted her at a table outside the main room. When I approached her, I was shocked and surprised by her appearance. She was drunk, perhaps even more drunk than the night she came to my apartment after her sister's birthday party. Her makeup was ruined, and she had too much lipstick on. Her friend was equally drunk and dressed like a barrio gangbanger. When she tried to introduce me to her friend, her speech was heavy and slurred. Nick approached us, and when he saw the scene, he suggested we leave right away. I told him I couldn't leave her like that. I told Andrea I'd take her home. She showered me with expletives and told me if I was ashamed of her, I could leave. People were looking at us, so I tried to be cool. Nick kept telling me to leave and forget about her. But I couldn't. She was practically living with me by then.

Eventually, her friend convinced her that she should listen to me and call it a night. It was a struggle to get her to my car. Nick was all kinds of displeased with me. He was adamant that I was making a mistake. After we put her in my car, he took me aside and told me I should open my eyes. He referred to them as "trash" and said I could do much better. His words stung, but rather than agree with him I kept searching for justifications. We said goodnight and promised to stay in touch.

Andrea fell asleep on the way home. I drove to my place and put her in bed. I then sat in my dark living room and tried to make sense of what had transpired. I needed someone to talk to. I knew the position of those close to me. I was the only dissenting voice. It was absolute madness.

The following day I had a conversation with Andrea and told her how disappointed I was with her behavior. I asked her if she felt she had a drinking problem. She assured me she didn't. She said she worked hard and was just having a little fun and couldn't understand my reaction. I wanted to believe her, so I let it go. I pretended like the incident had never happened.

Weeks later, I received a call from her telling me she'd found a room that she could afford and was leaving her mom's house. She wanted me to help move her stuff. I was surprised by the development but didn't ask any questions.

Her mom owned a house in East San Diego near the intersection of Highway 15 and University Avenue. She ended up with the house after her divorce from an alcoholic Army veteran. As I parked the car she came out of the house and met Andrea in the front yard. Andrea told her she'd come for her stuff. An argument ensued as they walked in the house. I stayed next to the car. I heard her mom say:

"*Quien es el cabron que trajistes contigo?*" (Who's the bastard you brought with you?)

"*Es mi novio.*" (He's my boyfriend.)

"*Madre de Dios! Con tantos muchachos Mexicanos decentes en el barrio tuvistes que escojer un Negro.*" (With so many decent Mexican boys in the neighborhood, you had to choose a Black guy.)

"*No es Negro, es Panameno y habla espanol.*" (He's not Black, he's Panamanian and he speaks Spanish.)

I helped Andrea put the stuff in the car. I had nothing to say to her mom.

She moved some stuff into this new place but actually spent very little time there. This prompted me to ask her how much she was spending for rent. After she told me, I made the comment that she should just completely move in with me and the money she was spending on that room could then be used for rent and food with me. She embraced the idea with enthusiasm. It was a done deal.

Of course, I didn't talk with my mom about this new arrangement. I felt it was my right to decide and she'd just have to adjust. The truth of the matter is that I'd fallen in love with an idea Nick came up with of us vacationing in Europe. I needed money for the trip, and this arrangement would give me an opportunity to save money. Had you asked me that at the time I would've denied it, of course.

Soon after she moved in for good, there was another drunken episode. I was home one night wondering where she was when the doorbell rang. When I opened the door, two other girls similar in appearance to the one I'd met on the double date, were dragging her up the stairs. They were laughing and cursing at her. I became angry. I told them to leave her and that they could go. Inside the room I went nuts on her. I yelled obscenities at her and grabbed her chin and kept screaming, "Look at you, look at you. You look like a whore." I slapped her once or twice. My mom came in and took me to her room. I was crying like a baby. I heard her leave and felt my world collapsing. I kept asking, "Why?!"

In the middle of my emotional meltdown, it didn't occur to me that I'd crossed a line by laying hands on Andrea. No, it was the furthest thing from my mind. In terms of relationships, I never cared that much before and was a bit confused about the amount of time and energy I was spending thinking about her. The days went by, and I kept hoping I'd hear from her, but there was nothing but silence on her end. Out of the blue, Richie showed up at my place for a surprise visit. We went for a drive, and I poured out my heart to him. So much was my distress that I never stopped to wonder if he was the best person to be talking to about my feelings. The accident with his brother had fractured our close relationship. I can't even remember how it was that he came to visit all of a sudden. Nevertheless, he did point out a few things to me that should've brought me back to reality.

He told me that he was surprised to see me in such a state. He said he'd seen me with better-looking and classier women and I never got myself all worked up about them. He reminded me that we were never about relationships but more about having fun and enjoying life. He said I needed to knock it off, stop acting like a wimp, and get my shit together. I heard everything he said, but the words didn't register in the decision-making hard drive. All I was thinking about was whether or not I should go try to find Andrea and talk things out with her.

Ultimately, that's exactly what I did. I found out she was staying with her aunt, so I went there. The aunt, righteously so, told me I wasn't welcome and should leave right away. I told her I wasn't looking for trouble and would leave if Andrea told me to leave. She said she'd let Andrea know I was there, and then closed the door on me. A few minutes later she opened the door again and let me in. Andrea walked out of the bedroom looking like she had a terrible hangover and not much sleep. It was obvious she'd been up all night and probably drank too much. Nothing had changed.

A straight-thinking man would've realized that it was time to move on. There was nothing to salvage there. Instead I found myself apologizing for my behavior and telling her I wanted her to come back to the apartment. The apology was no doubt a good thing. But asking her to return to the apartment with me was just plain dumb. That she agreed to return is equally puzzling, especially since her aunt, who'd been nearby listening to our conversation, flat out told her not to do so.

When she showed up at my place a day or so later, the look on my mom's face didn't require words. Nick came by and asked if I needed my head examined. I deflected all criticism and advice. I told Nick we should focus on putting the final touches on our trip to Europe. The malaise that'd been hanging over me disappeared and I felt myself breathing again. I convinced myself that everything was going to be okay because I would will it to be. To hell with all the naysayers.

The storm passed, and things settled down. All my energy and attention were dedicated to preparing for my European vacation. It appeared that my mom and Andrea were getting along okay. I really didn't know because I avoided any inquiries for fear that the truth would suck. Prior to leaving, I asked Andrea to be responsible and take care of things while I was gone. I told her my mom would need help shopping for groceries and running other errands. I gave her one of my credit cards and told her she could use it only in the event of an emergency. Looking back now I remember a lack of enthusiasm and sort of resignation underscoring my trip, especially coming from my mom who seemed like she had plenty to say but didn't want to rock the boat.

I spent the summer of 1985 visiting Italy and France. There were good moments and also bad ones. Nick and I couldn't agree on how to spend our time. He was from Europe so doing the tourist thing didn't appeal to him. I wanted to see and visit all the famous and historic places. Things got so bad that eventually we agreed to go our separate ways. What had started as a dream vacation—two buddies traveling through Europe laughing and having the time of their lives—fizzled into days and nights of wandering around Europe with no one to talk to or share things.

Trying to change that, one night I walked into a bar and tried to make friends with a group of Spaniards who seemed to be having a good time. I made contact in Spanish and was invited to have a drink. Next thing I know I was asked where I was from. I proudly replied I was from the States. Big mistake. These people collectively hated America and Yankee imperialism. The verbal attacks became so aggressive I feared for my safety. Without finishing the drink, I excused myself and left the bar. What a horrible experience!

My last days in Rome, I signed up for common bus tours and did the tourist thing. I felt so lonely and alone I swore I'd never make that mistake again. The next time I went some place I would go with someone who shared my vision and passion and was willing to create "feel good" lasting memories.

Nevertheless, the memories from this vacation remain, and the positive aspects are worth focusing on. From my arrival at Rome's Leonardo da Vinci International Airport to the train ride to Bari, there was no denying I was experiencing something different. On the bus from the airport to the train station I kept trying to make out what the locals were saying. I loved listening to the back and forth. The chatter sounded musical in a way. I felt the heat of the warm weather and marveled at the scenery.

At the train depot, hungry and thirsty, I could not get over the fact I could not find a spot that sold pizza. I smiled at the irony. The train ride to Bari was trying. We literally travelled like sardines in a can. And were ill prepared for the long distance. Finding water to drink and a place to pee proved a challenge. But the stay at Bari was superb. The family that received us treated us regally and refused monetary compensation. I would've gladly spent the entire vacation right there. I ate like I'd never eaten before and visited local tourist attractions. A professional motorcycle racer gave me a ride at speeds that made me blind. It was better than a rollercoaster. And on a dare from Nick I even jumped naked into the Adriatic Sea.

Back west we visited Sorrento and Capri and made lots of friends at the camping site we stayed at. I still have those pictures and looking at them evokes warm thoughts. Another train ride took us north to Ventimiglia on our way to Naples, France. In Monaco I visited the Monte Carlo casino. I could not afford to gamble, but it's a site to see. The building is a work of art, and besides the casino it's home to opera and ballet. The changing of the guards at the palace was also worth seeing. I will never forget the view of the yachts at Monte Carlo harbor off Rue Grimaldi. In Nice I bought souvenirs, which I took back as mementos.

I returned to Rome by myself, and there I took time to visit the Colosseum, Sistine Chapel, St. Peter's Basilica, and the Fontana di Trevi. For what it's worth I did toss my three coins into the fountain. Sadly, the legend did not prove true for me. Walking through the Colosseum gave me the sensation I'd been there before.

Michelangelo's work on the ceiling of the Sistine Chapel blew me away as did the size of the sculptures at the Basilica. I found the narrative of the guides fascinating as well as walking the grounds of historical sites that up to that point I'd only read about in school texts.

One of the last things I did was visit the ruins of Pompeii. I tried to imagine what it must have felt like on the eve of destruction. Unlike my time in Sorrento, I do not have pictures of these days. I was with a crowd but alone. I walked and listened, lost in my own thoughts, trying to convince myself that I was happy.

I spoke to Andrea on the phone several times while away. Of course, I pretended like I was having a wonderful time. She reported that things at home were fine. My mom would later contradict that by telling me that since the day I left Andrea hadn't been back to the apartment. Mom had been getting by on her own.

Andrea agreed to pick me up at LAX. When I arrived, she told me she had a surprise. My heart sunk. I just knew it wouldn't be anything good. Sure enough, Andrea had used my credit card to buy herself a used 208ZX sports car. I tried hard but couldn't hide my disappointment. She tried hard to convince me that it would all work out, but I wasn't having any of it. I rained on her parade.

9

I went to work, trying to undo the deal with the car.

I consulted with Pedro about the sales contract, and he assured me that she'd been taken to the cleaners. He went to his dealership, and according to him he did all he could to get me a better deal. I say this because from one used car salesman to another…who knows who's telling the truth? In the end, the whole thing ended up costing me a pretty penny. The 280ZX was replaced by a run-of-the-mill Buick Regal, which I was able to pay off on the spot. Andrea wasn't happy with what I'd done. Especially since all the while I was working to undo her deal I went ahead and leased a brand-new BMW 350 for myself.

I tried to pacify her by telling her she could drive the BMW anytime. The problem was the car was a stick shift and she could only drive automatic. I took her to the park a couple of times and tried to teach her, but she couldn't get the hang of it. Every time she stalled the car or grinded the gears, I would worry that the car would suffer irreparable damage. I finally nixed the idea of teaching her altogether. She resented this and stayed mad a long time.

I'd returned from Europe in September of 1985. A couple of months had gone by. We were entering the last quarter of 1985 and still trying to work through the bad feelings that the car situation had created when Andrea informed me she was pregnant.

I was stunned by the news. I suppose the look on my face wasn't one of delight but one of absolute terror instead. She took notice of this.

I struggled to find a good response to the news. When I spoke, I said all the wrong things. I intimated that I'd be supportive should she decide to have an abortion. Andrea blew her top. She flat out told me she was having the baby with or without my support. I had so many concerns about this I was having trouble articulating my feelings. I feared she had an unaddressed drinking problem and worried how this would impact the baby. Of course, she didn't think she had a drinking problem. The news was well-received by her part of the family. My mom was neutral. My friends thought it spelled trouble.

I'd been through a couple of situations already where abortions took center stage. As a Catholic, I believed this to be wrong and my conscience was bothering me. I wondered if this was God giving me another chance to get it right. I was hard on myself for having unprotected sex with Andrea while neglecting to define the nature of our relationship. I briefly wondered what if everyone was right about Andrea and me and I was wrong. In the end, I extracted a weak promise from her to quit drinking while pregnant or run the risk of ruining the baby, and then I fully embraced the idea of finally becoming a father.

News of the baby changed a lot of things. It was like everyone stopped focusing on self and shifted focus to the baby. Andrea took pregnancy seriously and followed medical advice to the letter. Just about every day I was getting schooled on something or the other that had to do with the baby. It was a time of peace and tranquility. All negativity was put on hold. It was a time to make plans and prepare for the future. Things at work were going well. I enrolled in college to get my degree with an eye on following up with law school.

I quietly began looking into the possibility of buying a home. When I found one that I liked and I was assured that there was real possibility I could get it, I shared the news with mom and Andrea. At first, the news was received with joy. Especially when they had an opportunity to see the place and agreed with me that it was nice. But all the goodwill and tranquility we had been experiencing came to a halt when Andrea demanded that her name be added to the deed. My mom objected vehemently to this demand, arguing that this was an opportunity for me to finally make good on my promise to buy her a house. Andrea, on the other hand, argued that she was protecting the baby's future.

Both women dug in on their views, and battle lines were drawn. People took sides, and everyone was in my ears telling me who was right and who was wrong and why. No matter whom I spoke to, a different point of view always surfaced. We were back to that feeling of unease and uncertainty. I confess I didn't know what was the right thing to do. I felt no matter what I decided someone was going to end up terribly unhappy.

In the end I decided that the only name that would appear on the deed would be my own. In working with the real estate agent, I realized that it was *my* credit that was being checked and *my* VA benefits that were being used. Neither the bank nor the real estate agent were asking me anything about my mom or Andrea. The only one responsible for making the payments was me, no one else.

When I announced my decision, the reaction was expected—massive disappointment all around. I tried to get both women to adapt a celebratory mood and concentrate on helping with the transition to our new home. But the negativity remained. I could sense the unhappiness and the ill feelings.

I continued to move forward with furnishing the place and preparing for the baby's arrival. As the due date drew near, animosity was put on hold and replaced by nervousness and anxiety. Andrea was way past her due date, and it looked like she was carrying twins even though we'd been assured that was not the case. It was July 1986, and my stress level was off the charts. But I didn't know it, and no one was checking up on me. I kept pushing as if all was okay, but deep down inside I wished I had a trusted confidant that could offer words of wisdom that might settle me down.

When I took Andrea to the hospital, I was full of trepidation. My mind drifted back to the beginning of the year when I was glued to the television set watching the Space Shuttle Challenger break apart after just 73 seconds into its flight. The craft disintegrated over the Atlantic Ocean with millions of unbelieving eyes witnessing the disaster. I took a deep breath and shook the vision of the smoke plume from my mind.

Things were not progressing as expected based on all that we'd learned at Lamaze classes. I won't try to offer a medical explanation here as that is way above my range of expertise. The bottom line is the baby was due but not coming out and Andrea was in a lot of pain. The doctors told me that we could wait a little longer for a natural birth or they could do surgery and deliver the baby that way. I opted for waiting until one of the doctors came and explained to me that if we waited any longer both Andrea and the baby would be at risk. So, surgery it was. I was given the option to be present in the operating room. I could observe what they were doing or sit at the head of the bed and hold Andrea's hand. I claimed I wanted to see everything.

The surgeon said okay, and then nodded at the nurse who positioned herself behind me. When the blood started coming out of the incision, I fainted. Thank goodness the nurse was right behind me to grab me. She walked me to a stool near the head of the bed and sat me there. I was a nervous wreck. I kept thinking something bad was about to happen.

When the baby was pulled out, another team of doctors went to work on him. He was purple and making no sound. I expected any moment they would tell me he was dead. Andrea kept asking if something was wrong. My voice trembled as I tried to reassure her that everything was okay. They told me to go with Andrea to the recovery room and someone would come talk to me soon. I asked if the baby was okay. One of the doctors told me there'd been complications but soon everything would be under control. He said not to worry.

In the recovery room my mind was spinning out of control. A million crazy things went through my head. I'd thought this was finally going to be a happy moment in my life. But it was anything but that. A little past the half hour, a doctor came into the recovery room with a smile on his face. He explained that the respiratory system had been blocked and they had to work to clear the airway so the baby could breathe. He further said the baby was in no danger, but they would keep him under observation to make sure. He said if I wanted, I could go with him to see the baby. When I saw him, he was huge. Normal color had returned to his skin and his little hands kept making a fist. He had pulled off the little blue cap they'd put on his head.

I stood there and stared at him for a long time until it hit me that there were others expecting an update on what had taken place. I presented the news in a positive way and kept to myself the anxious moments. I thanked God silently and made all kind of promises to Him that I'd later forget.

There is a reason why *Top Gun* is one of my all-time favorite movies. It was released May 1986 and was still going strong when my boy showed up.

10

As every new parent knows, the weeks following baby's arrival are difficult ones.

There are massive adjustments that have to be made. I continued to work and attend college as I was close to getting my degree. Getting up in the middle of the night to change diapers and feed the baby meant I wasn't getting enough rest. I was irritable and moody. When situations were brought to my attention, I'd become agitated and try to fix them as quickly as possible. My patience was short, and I wasn't prone to much discussion.

I guess mom was taking notice of all that was happening, and she quietly made arrangements to return to Philadelphia. When she broke the news to me, she caught me by surprise. I tried to object, but it was a done deal. When I took her to the airport, I felt like I was losing the one person that I completely trusted to have my back—ironic, since up to that point I'd not done anything to help her feel that way.

With Andrea returning to work, we started with the babysitter carousel. We had problems finding a reliable and dependable person. This opened the door for one of Andrea's "cousins" to take the job as a live-in babysitter. Initially this seemed like a good deal, but later it would prove a terrible mistake. Her name was Norma, and while I didn't know this at the time she was hired, she was from the same town in Mexico where Andrea's family was from. She was very close to Andrea's mom and took the job on her suggestion. So while before it was me, my mom, Andrea, and Junior—now it was me, Norma, Andrea, and Junior. Like I said, this made it so that I had a spy living under my roof. I discovered later that she was reporting daily to Andrea's mom about all that was happening in my home and passing on to Andrea "suggestions" from her mom.

I'd not had sex with Andrea since before Junior's arrival. I tried to be sensitive about her recovery time and asked her to let me know when she'd been cleared by her doctor. She had a thousand reasons and excuses why sex was off the table for the foreseeable future. I became extremely frustrated with this situation. When an opportunity came up for me to have a date with a nurse I'd met at one of the hospitals I visited while on patrol, I took advantage of it. No doubt this was an error in judgment on my part. Especially since because that one date had been a success, I didn't see any need to stop. The floodgates had opened. I didn't trouble Andrea anymore. It was like I was living with a roommate and nothing more.

If she noticed the change, she didn't say. We both went about our business with little, if any, communication. On weekends she wanted me to go with her to her mom's place, but I always found an excuse not to go. I was happier doing things on my own. This didn't sit well with her, but that didn't bother me.

Given the situation that I just described, it would appear that talk of marriage didn't make any sense. But obviously what I was thinking and seeing wasn't the same thing that Andrea was thinking and seeing. Junior was born July 1986. I received my Bachelor's degree January 1987 and immediately began the process to enroll in law school. I secured the needed recommendations and completed the necessary paperwork. I was set to go. I was back on track and moving forward with my dream. It was then that, unexpectedly, Andrea brought up the subject of marriage.

I'd been minding my own business, not paying much attention to her, and she seemed okay with that. There were zero complaints on her part and no indication she even noticed the ocean divide that existed between us. However, as my graduation day approached, I started to notice little improvements in her attitude and small relationship gestures. For instance, she wanted me to help her file for citizenship, and sex had returned to the bedroom although somehow it felt different now. It was during one of these moments, with the holidays right on top of us, that the subject of marriage was first brought up.

I was introduced to the subject in a casual and off-handed way. And I was still thinking about whether or not this was something I wanted to do when I discovered that plans were being formulated as if it were a done deal. It was like I had no say in the matter. And I didn't. Andrea and her mom took charge of organizing everything.

As they say, all I had to do was show up and bring my wallet.

When I broke the news to my mom and the handful of people that formed my social circle, they were incredulous. *No one* thought this was a good idea. I was back to feeling the way I felt when I first met Andrea. It was me and her against the world. This wasn't true, but still it made me mad. Rather than take time to listen and reevaluate things, I isolated myself and surrendered to whatever Andrea (and her mom) decided to do.

We had to jump through some hoops with the Catholic Church, but eventually we got married in June of 1987. Junior was baptized at the same time. There were dozens of guests in attendance both at church and at the reception. But besides the four or five people that came at my invitation, everyone else was a stranger to me. When I look at the pictures that were taken that day, I can now see the lack of joy and happiness. What I see in my face is stress and someone going through the motions. Interestingly, one of my female guests took me to the dancefloor, and while we were dancing, she asked to see my wedding band. When I showed it to her, she wanted to know why I was wearing it on my right hand. I was flabbergasted. She discreetly switched the ring to my left hand while trying to hide her concern for the meaning of that omen.

The wedding reception was held at the house of Andrea's mom. I pretty much sat at a table on the perimeter of the festivities with the few friends that were there as my guests. I wasn't paying any attention to what Andrea was up to. We had tickets to the Bahamas for our honeymoon, and I was just waiting for the moment the limousine would take us to the airport. When we got in the limo, I immediately noticed Andrea was inebriated. I became angry but held my tongue. However, my mood had soured and I kept my distance. Who acts like that on their wedding day? Was I wrong?

At the airport, my mood didn't improve. Andrea separated herself from me and stayed on the pay phone, presumably with her mother. In theory, this was supposed to be one of the happiest days of my life. Why did it feel otherwise?

On the plane to Miami Andrea ordered herself a cocktail. I gave her a look, but she wasn't moved by that. When we got to Miami she wanted to sit at the bar while we waited for the connecting flight. That's when I spoke my mind. Her response to my concerns was that she had just gotten married and she was celebrating. She wanted to know what was wrong with me. I brought up the promise she made not to drink anymore. She countered that she had kept her promise and didn't drink while pregnant. I didn't want to make a scene, so I let it be.

We didn't talk on the way to the Bahamas. There were no public displays of affection, no holding hands, no outward signs that we'd just been married. Things couldn't have been more catastrophic.

When we arrived at the hotel, she complained it was a dump. She was expecting a five-star hotel by the beach. We'd be there all week, but she refused to unpack her suitcase. She found fault with everything and wanted me to try to get us a room at one of the big hotels we'd passed by during the taxi ride. I told her she was crazy. I tried to explain to her that between the wedding reception and the trip, all my savings were gone. She suggested I use my credit cards. The more we talked, the more I started to wonder who this person was I'd just married. She wanted to play rich and didn't care about the consequences.

That night when I tried to make love to her, she refused me. She complained she had a headache and didn't want to be bothered. She had her back to me, so I pulled her by the shoulder and forced her to look at me. I told her she was full of shit and playing games. She cursed at me, and I slapped her. I called her a bitch, a whore, and any other filthy word that came to my mind. She responded in kind with similar foul language.

I left the room and went to the hotel lobby to clear my head. This was a nightmare of epic proportions. I needed to talk to someone, but who?

The rest of the week fell into a sad routine. There was very little talking. Any questions asked were met with "yes," "okay," or "no" answers. We slept in the same bed without touching each other. She'd get up first and head for breakfast without waiting for me. We'd then go to the beach with no particular agenda in mind. I'd get in the ocean and try to enjoy the beauty of the place, the warm water—but my heart was troubled, and joy escaped me.

There were no pictures taken, no fun things done together.

We were both just waiting for the flight back to California. A couple of days before leaving she said she wanted to go shopping for gifts. This resulted in more aggravation because I refused to pay for the stuff she bought.

The flight back was more of the same. I don't know what was going through her mind, but I know I felt like the biggest fool to ever walk the face of the earth. I kept replaying in my mind all that had taken place since I met her. I was afraid to reach any strong conclusions, but it was hard to find love and affection and togetherness, unity, joy, happiness, and what have you. I wondered if all that was happening was my fault. Based on my attitudes and beliefs, on the kind of man I wanted to be and the kind of family I wanted to have, I was falling way short. I'd been rushing from one thing to another without pausing and carefully examining where I was heading. My pride and ego kept me from listening to the advice others were giving me, and now I was in over my head. I kept coming back to the notion that I'd done what was right by my son so he could have what we didn't have—a stable family environment. A mother and father he could count on. But even this rationale wasn't enough to justify the reality of my situation. This marriage was a failure, and it'd just begun. Or was it? Could it be that this was just a bump in the road?

Upon my return from the fiasco that was my honeymoon, I determined to keep things to myself and focus on work and school. I felt that if I buried myself in those priorities, things would just work themselves out. I wasn't sure what exactly that would look like, but I didn't feel the need to think about it too much. I had my obligations to keep me entertained and my son as a distraction. He was a good-looking baby, and I enjoyed taking him around with me while I ran errands. I also had the tennis club and Toastmasters for good measure. I hung around the house long enough to pay bills and get a little rest. I was a man on the move.

The frozen tundra that was my home thawed out a little when Andrea announced that she intended to apply for the Sheriff Academy and could use my help. She'd achieved citizenship, so the path was cleared for her to pursue her dream. There was no family discussion over pros and cons. She had decided, and that was that.

11

Even though the pursuit of her new career made it possible for us to have more interaction, I secretly wasn't pleased with the decision-making process. We weren't working as a unit. There was no family spirit. I knew of her long-time desire to join the law enforcement community, so this shouldn't have been a surprise. Still, it felt like another indication that she really didn't give a damn about what I thought or felt.

I'm sure that to those who came around us it looked like we were getting along and we were executing a great game plan. But the truth was we were two individuals pulling in separate directions, pursuing different goals, in a sort of détente.

A few months after we came back from the Bahamas, around October 1987, with the bitter taste of the honeymoon still in my mouth, my old Marine Corps buddy Richie came to visit and spend some time with me. We'd been through a lot, and our relationship had suffered since the car accident with his brother. But that said, I was really happy to see him and have him as my guest. I wanted to run a few things by him, get some feedback. This was an opportunity to get some things off my chest and do some catching up. We'd just get dressed and hit the town like in the old days. It was a beautiful Southern California day.

As we proceeded with the plan, Andrea announced that she was coming with us. I was caught off guard and totally surprised by her reaction. We hadn't been going anywhere together.

Richie and I tried to play it off. But no matter how much I tried to explain to her that I needed this time with my friend, she wouldn't budge. I became very angry with her. Richie then said to me that it was no big deal and if she wanted to ride with us it was okay. I was pissed. She took the baby to a neighbor, and we left. We went to a miniature golf place and tried to have some fun but to no avail. Andrea was determined to be a party pooper no matter what was suggested. I was so upset I started to feel sick. My blood pressure was probably sky high. I told Andrea we were leaving. Now even though up to that point she had refused to play any of the games, she said she wasn't ready to go. I became unglued. I grabbed her hands and started dragging her towards the car. In the parking lot, I kicked her in the ass.

Richie was shocked. He pleaded with me to get a hold of myself and cool off. We rode home in silence. At the house, things became awkward. Richie wanted to leave, but I insisted he stay. I told him we would eat something and then leave. Andrea took advantage of the opportunity to tell Richie what a big asshole I was. I was lost in my own thoughts trying to understand what was happening to me. I wanted to respond to some of the things she was saying but felt emotionally exhausted. I kept quiet and went about getting dressed so Richie and I could leave the house again.

When I was ready to go, I motioned to Richie who was busy trying to keep the peace. Andrea went nuts again and said we weren't going anywhere without her. I told her she needed to stay home and take care of the baby. She didn't want to hear that. She took my car keys and stood in front of the door to block our path. She was furious and cursing up a storm.

She threatened to slash the tires on my BMW. I lost my patience with her and tried to wrestle the car keys away from her. Richie stood by unable to believe his eyes. When I at last pried the keys from her hands, she fell to the ground crying and cursing.

Richie and I left the house, but the mood had soured even more. I drove around aimlessly. I was driving by a public park, so I veered into it and parked the car.

We sat for a long moment without saying anything. I wanted to talk but didn't know where to start. Richie spoke first and said all the things you'd expect him to say. He was blown away by what he'd witnessed and expressed deep disappointment with my actions. He said something to me that I never forgot. He said that he would never lay hands on a woman, no matter what, and if anyone had touched his mom? He would kill him.

When I heard that, I thought to myself that he didn't know the bed of misery I'd made for myself. I wanted to tell him that I really believed I was doing the right thing by standing by her and the baby and that in my heart I felt we could make things work. But these thoughts didn't make any sense when contrasted with the perspective he presented. To protect myself I concluded that he didn't understand what was going on. We continued to talk way past the midnight hour. Mostly we talked about how things used to be and what we hoped life would turn out to be.

As we drove back to the house, I had a terrible premonition. I had this uneasy feeling that I couldn't shake. When we walked in the house, I saw a note from a police officer stating Andrea had filed a police report on me. I needed to contact Internal Affairs as soon as possible.

Richie got up early Sunday morning and left. It was like he was trying to get away from us, from me, as quickly as possible. The visit did nothing to repair our fractured friendship. If anything, it made matters worse.

He refused to testify at my trial. The next time I saw him I was wearing a prison uniform.

After Richie left, I told Andrea we needed to talk. I told her she had made a mistake in calling the cops. I made it clear to her that if I got fired, our standard of living would suffer. There was no telling where we'd end up. I didn't apologize for my behavior. I proceeded to paint as gloomy a picture of the future as I could. I asked her if she thought she could pay all the bills on her own because she surely wouldn't be getting any money from me. What impact would this have on the pursuit of her new career? Was she aiming for a divorce?

She didn't answer, but I could tell she was thinking.

Internal Affairs sustained the complaint against me. I was reprimanded and ordered to seek family therapy. I caught a break as the department chose to keep things in house and there was no referral to the District Attorney's office. This was due in large part to the fact that when Andrea was contacted by investigators she refused to cooperate.

A couple of things are worth noting at this point. I don't think this would've happened in today's climate. It's safe to say that the department later came to regret this decision. But most importantly, Andrea would probably be alive today had she followed through and cooperated with investigators. Our relationship was broken and beyond repair, but neither one of us was willing to admit that and act accordingly. We had concluded that it was better to keep up appearances and live at risk than to do the right thing. I wasn't willing to admit that I had a problem and kept blaming everything on her. She wasn't willing to look out for herself and abandon ship no matter what the cost. Resentment would continue to fester unabated on both sides.

This resentment was exacerbated at the family therapy sessions. The therapist wouldn't allow me to speak and instead gave Andrea free reign to unload on me. She was vicious in her assessment of me as a man, a husband, a human being. I felt embarrassed and humiliated. I was angry when I left the session and didn't speak to her for a long time. We did manage to book another appointment, but I wasn't looking forward to that.

The second session began with more of the same, so rather than trying to defend myself this time I disengaged and just ignored them. When we left the session, I didn't bother to hang around to book another appointment. I was done.

In the aftermath of what had transpired, I was spooked. I kept telling myself that I needed to focus on what I was trying to accomplish and ignore the little things. I kept pretending that all was well and put on a good front. I refused to take a look at myself and explore the issues and resentment I was living with and the fact that I was normalizing domestic violence.

It was somewhere in this time frame that I met Joan. She was an educator assigned to help with a job I was doing for the department. As a young woman she'd played the part of Snow White at Disneyland. We met in Los Angeles while attending training with LAPD. She seemed like a fun lady and was easy to talk to. She was a welcome distraction from all the upheaval I'd been experiencing lately. We became fast friends. She was married with two children. She thought it would be a good idea for Andrea and me to visit her and her husband upon our return home. I wasn't feeling good about that idea but went along with it to keep from having to explain too much this early in our friendship.

Before that happened though, we ended up sleeping together. Joan became part of my daily life. I'd see her at work and off duty also. Sometimes she'd visit me at school on the nights I had classes. She was a social butterfly and often organized activities for couples in her social circle. These were mostly educators, people she worked with. When I told Andrea that we'd been invited to one of those activities, I didn't think she'd want to attend since we weren't on good terms, but to my surprise she was willing to go.

When Joan met Andrea, she quickly went to work on gaining her trust and confidence. I wasn't sure what Joan was up to, but I sat back and just let it play out. So it was that Andrea and I were incorporated into this circle and began attending activities with them from time to time.

On one occasion, we travelled north with the group to spend time at a resort playing tennis. During the Christmas holidays we spent time in the mountains enjoying the snow and cold weather with Joan and her husband. On the surface it looked like we were trying to salvage our relationship by doing things together, but it was all a ploy orchestrated by Joan so she and I could spend time together. It looked like Andrea enjoyed talking to and doing things with Joan.

They even began to talk on the phone. Joan would call me to set up a date, and then ask me to put Andrea on the phone and they'd talk for a few minutes. And so it was that it never looked suspicious whenever Joan would call me at home. It didn't matter who was listening. I was free to take the call without reservations, announce who was calling, and then hand the phone to Andrea.

As Super Bowl day was on the horizon, the planning for a get-together at Joan's place intensified. Andrea was busy preparing to attend the academy and saying goodbye to her old job. Our relationship remained on ice, as we really hadn't taken time to sit down and talk about the things that had gone on between us. We were both ignoring the elephant in the room. I was giddy with this thing I had with Joan, and my focus was on school and work.

On party day, things began a little shaky. As soon as we arrived, Joan handed Andrea a glass of wine. I was going to say something but remembered Joan was in the dark about this issue. Andrea took the wine and started mingling. There were lots of people in attendance. Joan was going back and forth and kept smiling and telling me to have fun. I was uneasy and feared a spectacle from Andrea.

After the game everyone stretched and headed for the door as the next day was a working day. Everyone except Andrea. She wanted more wine. And Joan kept giving her more. I told Joan she'd had enough, but her not knowing the history she kept telling me it was okay. It was midnight when I put my foot down and said we had to go. Joan's husband was asleep on the couch. Andrea was falling down drunk.

On the way home I couldn't help myself. As soon as we were alone, I began to lecture her. I told her she was a disgrace and an embarrassment. I cursed at her and called her names. She responded by turning the radio on at full volume. I tried to turn it down, and she slapped my hand away and turned it back up. I went for the knob again and again. She pushed my hand away. Then she tried to scratch my face. I almost lost control of the vehicle. I pulled over to the curb and asked if she was out of her mind. She didn't respond. She wasn't crying. She had that intoxicated look on her face and seemed ready to fight. I looked at her for a long moment, and then got back on the road. We rode in silence the rest of the way.

When I pulled into the garage and stopped the car, she got out and left in her car before I could close the garage door. It was late, and I had to work the next day, so I went to bed thinking she'd be back any moment. However, when the alarm woke me up, I realized she was still gone.

I went to work wondering where she'd gone (I never learned the answer to that question). I called Joan and asked her to meet me as soon as she could. When we met, I told her what had happened after we left her home. She asked me if I wanted her to try to reach Andrea and find out what was going on. I told her that was okay with me.

Later that day, Joan called to tell me that Andrea agreed to return home if she (Joan) could be present to serve as a mediator. I agreed, and so it was that she came back home. What I remember the most about that evening is that Andrea kept saying she wanted me to stop telling her how to live her life. Joan was in a hurry to get home, so she kept trying to get assurances that all would be well once she left. I told her not to worry and thanked her for taking the time.

I wasn't about to say or do anything. My mind was wondering if Andrea had determined to move out and move on. I wanted to get clarification from her, but I didn't want to start an argument and was afraid of what she might say. If she had, how would everything play out?

The other thing that was on my mind was the warning I'd received that if the police came to my home again, I was toast. Paralyzed by fear, I then proceeded to go about my business as if all was well. I tried hard to put on a good face, but the tension in the air was palpable. I don't know if Andrea said anything to the babysitter or she could tell that things were not well between us, but thinking back now I believe she was aware and they were definitely talking about things.

Whatever they would discuss, I wasn't in the loop anymore. This would prove critical later. Valentine's Day came and went, but it had nothing to do with us. There was a heavy fog over our home and no sunshine in the horizon. I should've asked for help from someone but kept silent instead. I felt indecisive and foolish.

Andrea acted as if I didn't exist.

12

We began the month of March 1988 as two strangers sharing the same roof.

We hardly spoke to one another. We'd get up in the mornings and go about the business of getting ready for work in silence. She'd head to the academy, and I'd report to work. I'd leave work, and then attend law school in the evening. I'd return home just before midnight, find her in bed sound asleep, oblivious to the world. I suspected she'd been drinking, makeup still on her face.

I was still seeing Joan, but the thrill was gone. I felt that there were things happening in my life that needed to be addressed. I just didn't know where to start or how to go about it. My pride and ego kept getting in the way. I kept thinking that the situation was my problem and I needed to solve it without outside assistance. Furthermore, I believed with all my heart that *she* was the problem, not me. One morning, she asked me to follow her to the mechanic because her car needed repairs.

She was going to drop the car off, and then I would take her to the academy. I got in my car ready to follow. Then I noticed something unusual. She had the babysitter and the baby get in the car with her. I thought about that as I followed them.

After leaving her car with the mechanic, they all jumped in my car for the rest of the trip. No one was speaking to me. I was just the driver. As we neared the site, she had me stop the car still a couple of blocks away. She said it was okay, that she wanted to walk the rest of the way. She said goodbye to the babysitter and the baby, and then reminded me of the time I should pick her up in the evening.

On the way back there was no attempt at small talk with the babysitter. Once home, I took the baby with me for a walk. In the afternoon I went for a drive and stopped by a car dealership to look at the latest models. I guess I was still thinking that things between Andrea and me would get better. I was delusional. The evidence was before me that there was no relationship anymore.

I can't remember how it was that the babysitter and the baby ended up going with me to pick up Andrea. Perhaps the babysitter suggested it. In any event, when we got to the academy, they were still doing physical exercises. We sat on the bleachers and waited. Andrea didn't acknowledge me.

When she joined us, she greeted the babysitter and picked up the baby. As we walked to the car, she told me one of her mates would be joining us. She said they'd be attending a party to celebrate their graduation. Before I could respond, the friend joined us and she turned her attention to her friend. She didn't introduce me to her friend. They ignored me. I was invisible. At the mechanic, they all got out and walked away without saying anything to me. This pissed me off. But any doubts I may have had were now clear. Andrea had a different mind-set. I no longer mattered.

I got home before them and was still feeling disrespected. I determined to speak to Andrea about how she was acting. However, her mate's presence and a telephone call I received from my mom prevented me from saying anything. She walked in, quickly changed, and left the house in a hurry. It was still daylight, and as she left she said she'd be back in a couple of hours. It was the babysitter's Friday, and she usually got a ride from Andrea to her place of residence on that day. I assumed that would be the case again.

Time passed, and it was now late evening. No sign of Andrea and zero communication. I told the babysitter I'd be taking her home and asked her to get the baby ready for bed. I waited for her, and after a while I noticed I couldn't hear any movement on her part. I called her name and asked her what was taking so long. Eventually she came downstairs with the baby and a handbag. I took her home. She rode in silence, and I meanwhile took time to express my frustration with Andrea.

I found out during my trial that the babysitter had been paid to work an extra day. When asked why she didn't tell me that on the night in question, she claimed she was afraid of me. I was blown away by her answer, but looking back now I can see that. I was in a bad mood.

Andrea returned home just past the ten o'clock hour. I was sitting in the living room with the TV on. I looked at her, and she was obviously drunk. She was having problems maintaining her balance. She walked past me and went into the bedroom without saying anything. I followed her and began verbally abusing her and pressing her for answers to my questions. She pleaded with me to leave her alone. I wouldn't. I worked myself up into a state of fury to the point of battering her. I kept her from calling the police and leaving the house.

She was furious and struck me in the face with a wind breaker that was laying on the bed. She said some mean things. She swore she would get even with me and "take me to the cleaners." She promised I would never see my son again and said that I was a fool. That she never really loved me. I kept her from taking a call that could've saved her life. The phone call caused me to pause and leave her alone. However, on my way out of the bedroom I saw the invitations to her impending graduation and I proceeded to tear them up. While I was busy doing that, she opened the cabinet where I kept my service revolver and armed herself. I just knew she was going to shoot me. Rather than running for cover, I charged at her to keep from getting shot.

We wrestled for control of the gun. I was behind her when I finally managed to pry the weapon from her hand. I was in a state of rage and began shaking her by the shoulders while asking her if she was crazy when I heard the gun go off. I stood up, dropped the gun, and went from rage to despair. I tried to get her to talk to me, but she was unresponsive and her body lifeless. I called 911, identified myself, and requested emergency assistance. The paramedics came and pronounced her dead.

I was arrested on the spot and taken to police headquarters for questioning. I waived my Miranda rights and gave a full statement. That statement was later used by the prosecution to secure a murder conviction.

The days following my arrest were dark and painful. I'd fallen off a cliff, and bottom was a long ways away. I wanted to die. It was the thought of my son asleep in the upstairs bedroom that kept me from killing myself. When police arrived at my home in response to the 911 call, I begged them to shoot me. I was placed in a patrol car with an officer standing guard. Feeling that my humanity was in jeopardy, I started talking uncontrollably, trying to make sense of the senseless.

Of course, everything I was saying was being recorded.

At the police station I waived my Miranda rights and continued talking nonstop. I knew the people that were questioning me and those observing the tragedy unfold, but the look on their faces said they didn't know me at all. This was just the beginning of what was to come.

I wasn't thinking straight and incapable of making decisions for myself, but no one cared about that. I was in bad shape when they took me into custody, and no one suggested I call a lawyer or contact a union rep. I was questioned from about midnight til daylight. I kept telling them that I was behind my wife when I wrestled the weapon from her hand and began shaking her by the shoulder violently when I heard the shot. I stood up and dropped the gun in disbelief. I immediately called 911. Yet, a Polaroid picture showed up in court of "me" standing over a model on her knees while pointing the gun at her head. Nothing like that happened. I was negligent and angry but had no desire to kill her. But through their actions they planted the seed in the prosecutor's mind that it was an execution-style killing. When they felt they had all the evidence they needed, they told me I'd be booked in jail on a murder charge.

At the jail, I was placed on suicide watch. I couldn't sleep. My soul and my spirit were in turmoil. I asked to speak to a priest. They wanted to know if I had someone in mind. I didn't, but then I thought about the priest that had married us. They said they'd reach out to him. I was crushed when I was informed that the priest refused to come see me.

The arraignment was like an out-of-body experience. The courtroom was packed. All eyes on me. The media showed up in droves. My mom said I looked pathetic and unrecognizable, like someone brought out of an insane asylum. I'm sure you've seen pictures on TV of perps wearing those baggie orange suits? Just close your eyes and imagine. I couldn't tell you what was said or what was discussed, nor who all was present. I suppose the transcripts could if they're still around.

Weeks later, I was released on bail thanks to my neighbors who came to my rescue. Eventually, I returned home to deal with the months of waiting for trial. I managed to keep custody of my son over my mother-in-law's strenuous objections, but during that time the mistakes and errors in judgment kept piling up.

My last paycheck was brought to my home by a community relations officer who told me in no uncertain terms not to go near the department for anything. From the time of my arrest going forward, no officer could be seen talking to me. In fact, a memo was circulated that I was to receive no assistance from anyone connected to the department or they ran the risk of being fired.

I needed to secure legal representation for my trial. After numerous attempts, Nick finally passed the bar exam. He represented me at the arraignment and wanted to assume responsibility for my defense. Considering he was fresh out of law school, this wasn't a good idea. I told him so, and his response was since I didn't trust him to go fuck myself. The Public Defender was ready to go, but I'd never heard of them winning a case, let alone a murder case. The next option was a lawyer Nick had introduced me to and who he referred to as a "buffoon." He was a Mexican by the name of Bautista. He specialized in plea-bargaining drug cases in federal court. He agreed to take my case and petitioned the court to be appointed. When people would ask who was representing me and I told them, they'd become speechless. But I had no money and therefore was stuck. In retrospect I should've taken my chances with the Public Defender's Office.

During a pretrial meeting at Bautista's office, his investigator showed me pictures of the party Andrea had attended and the autopsy report. The pictures gave the impression that couples were gathered around a large table with plenty of alcohol on it. The people were very close to one another with their arms resting on each other's shoulders. The investigator asked me if I thought Andrea was having an affair. I said I didn't know.

Next, he showed me the autopsy report. I was stunned when I saw that at the time of death she had a .26% BAC (Blood Alcohol Concentration). To this day I just don't know how she wasn't stopped for DUI on the way home and more impressively managed to park the car in the garage without hitting anything. The report also indicated the presence of opiates in her system and semen in her vagina. I didn't know how to process all this information. Based on my reaction, Bautista decided not to pursue the issue. From the pictures I saw, the only person who appeared at my trial was the woman who came to the house with Andrea.

Within a year I was prosecuted and convicted of murdering my wife. There were two trials. The first one ended in a hung jury after an acquittal of First-Degree Murder. Eight African Americans felt this was a crime of passion that belonged in the manslaughter category. The remaining four White jurors were adamant about Second-Degree Murder. The judge at my first trial allowed many character witnesses in my defense. The judge at the second trial did not allow any character witnesses and the prosecutor got away with empaneling an all-White jury composed of mostly women to sit in judgment. They reached a verdict in a record thirty minutes. It took them longer to decide who would be the jury forewoman. Bautista had fallen asleep at the wheel.

Thinking back, prior to the first trial, I'd hired a Mexican woman named Lola to do domestic work at my house. She was to clean and get rid of things that would be of no use to me going forward. One day, while she was cleaning the baby's room she found bottles of booze stashed in the closet behind boxes and items of clothing. I told Bautista about the discovery, and he indicated that the autopsy report made the point. Lola and I spoke a little about my situation, which she no doubt knew something about because of the local publicity. During the conversation, Lola asked if I'd be willing to see a spiritualist. She said she knew a lady in Tijuana that was good at doing "*limpias*" (spiritual cleansing), and she worked strictly on donations. I said I guess—heck, why not? Together we travelled to the heart of Tijuana to a very poor and run-down neighborhood where flies, garbage, and stray dogs and cats decorated the area. The homes were nothing but shacks that looked like they'd come apart any moment. I asked her if it was safe to leave the car unattended. She said not to worry. We went downhill following a beaten path and came upon a line of people waiting to see the spiritualist. I was not sure I wanted to wait in line. I felt like a fish out of water. I was anxious and looking around for danger. I wondered about the sanity of this undertaking.

Lola told me to relax, that she'd talk to the spiritualist's associates and explain my situation. I was allowed to go ahead of the others. The spiritualist put me in a circle of fire. There were candles all over the room and images of saints. Also, lots of fresh flowers, which gave the room a sweet fragrance. She did not ask any questions. She was a middle-aged woman with pleasant features, covered from head to toes with what appeared to be a white sheet. There were two other women in the room with us. They did not speak or look at me. Their heads were down, lips were moving as if praying. The spiritualist walked around me and sprinkled what seemed like water over my body as she whispered something I could not understand. Finally, she broke a couple of eggs and put them in a glass of water. She then had me step out of the circle and holding my hands palms up she told me someone had done something wicked and evil to me but that the expected results had backfired because there was another spirit looking out for me. She gave me instructions on things to do to undo the evil spell. With the help of Lola, I did as instructed. I visited her twice more before the trial.

After the first trial, I forgot about the spiritualist. More so since Lola became upset with me for taking her niece out on a date, and she then cut me loose.

I received a life sentence with the possibility of parole as mandated by the California Penal Code.

The only officers that showed at my trial were ones there to testify against me. They wouldn't even look me in the eyes. And it didn't stop there. Years later, when I started attending parole hearings, the letters from the department opposing parole were the most vicious and filthy.

Payback? Who knows.

13

When you're pulled out of a jail cell in the dark hours of the morning, placed in handcuffs and leg restraints, and put on a bus with other convicted felons, destination prison, your thoughts shift from what you did to what's going to happen to you. You don't see anyone crying on that bus. You see mean, angry faces. Some of these men will be predators, others prey.

You need to decide quickly what side of the fence you want to be on. I'm not a tough guy, not by any stretch of the imagination. But since I'd thought about killing myself several times, I silently made up my mind that I would die defending myself before becoming prey. When I heard some cons speaking Spanish on the bus, an idea began to formulate in my mind: As much as possible I would adapt the persona of just another immigrant caught up in the system. I'd speak English only when necessary and gravitate towards Central, South American, and Caribbean inmates. I had no idea how this was going to play out, but I convinced myself that this was the safest approach as I learned about life in my new environment.

I was transported to the Richard J. Donovan facility in San Diego. I was immediately placed in the hole for my own protection. The local news had not done me any favors. The place was a madhouse. The inmates slept all day and stayed up all night yelling back and forth. I wondered if that was how I was going to do my time and whether or not I could handle that. No one spoke to me, and I had no concept of what prison life was like. Finally, after a couple of weeks I was taken before a classification committee where I was told they would send me to San Luis Obispo.

At the Colony, the first few months were the worst. Guys were always making challenging remarks whenever I walked by. Mostly they wanted to know how it felt to be on the other side. And whether or not I still felt like a tough guy without the badge and the gun. One day I was standing in line waiting for the shower. A young gay guy from the surrounding area doing a short time pulled me to the side. At first, I thought he was coming with some funny business. I was ready to tell him where he could go when he began to school me about the Colony. He said that as long as I didn't initiate a fight no one was going to touch me. However, if I lost my cool and took a swing at someone, they were going to try to kill me before the guards could stop them. He said most, if not all, the inmates housed at this facility were there on protective custody. He mentioned the names of some famous guys, including two members of the Manson Family who were housed in another yard. I took all this in without any comment. I don't remember the fellow's name, but he also promised that as long as he was on the tier he would walk me to chow and would have my back if it became necessary.

I didn't admit this to him, but I was secretly pleased. Unfortunately for me he paroled not long after that and I never saw him again.

After he left, and in keeping with the plan I'd begun to formulate on the bus ride, I joined the crowd watching some Hispanic inmates playing soccer. I stood by and watched silently. I wasn't sure if they knew anything about me but decided it was time to find out what kind of reception I would get from them. A tall Mexican inmate that was giving instructions approached me and asked in Spanish if I could play. I told him I played growing up in Panama. He then introduced me to the other players as "Panama," and told me to pick out a pair of soccer shoes and join the practice. From that day on my new handle was "Panama" and I was a soccer player. This did not stop some from whispering and saying things when I walked by, but since I kept ignoring the taunts and worked hard to become an integral part of the soccer team eventually the storm passed. I also began to put my bilingual skills to use for the benefit of the Hispanic community. I refused any compensation, and whenever possible I treated the fellows to a soda from the canteen.

In prison, being nice to people doesn't guarantee safety. Character does. You learn to mind your own business. See no evil, hear no evil, do no evil. You stay away from guards lest you get labeled a snitch. If you must talk about yourself, you keep it simple and don't elaborate. Most cons won't ask questions because they don't want you asking questions about them.

During this period of adjustment, I found comfort in the promises of my trial lawyer that the appellate court would overturn my conviction on the grounds of prosecutorial misconduct. When I met my appellate lawyer, that possibility became less certain.

She was a family law practitioner with no experience in criminal law. When I read her appellate brief, my concerns deepened. I closed my eyes and asked myself what judge in the community where I came from would reverse my conviction based on what she wrote. The answer was none. And time would prove me right.

While I waited for the legal process to run its course, I was assigned to work in the dining hall. The job consisted mainly of cleaning tables, sweeping, and mopping. I had to be there for all three meals. The position had no pay number. In the mornings, the first inmates to show up for breakfast were the ones that worked at PIA (Prison Industry Authority). Old cons joked that these were the big money guys. In prison a job is important even if it doesn't pay. That's because those who work are issued a red privilege card, and those that don't a blue one. This comes into play for just about every aspect of life behind walls. It impacts visiting, canteen, access to the library, telephone calls, hobby, laundry, yard time, and participation in sports.

Inmates that worked without pay made up the difference by stealing anything they could from the job site and selling the stuff on the yard. Risky business for sure, but the prevailing attitude was, *What are they going to do to me? Put me in prison?* Followed by a hearty laugh.

I spoke to a few of the guys that worked at PIA and got the rundown on how to go about applying for a job there. Everything was contingent on how well I performed on the TABE test (Test of Adult Basic Education) administered by the education department. If I didn't show I could read and write at least to an eighth-grade level I could not work in PIA. I would be put in school to improve my score. I aced the test, or to put it another way I got the highest score I could get. The test proved I could read and write to the level of a high school graduate. Of course, all this could've been avoided had I been able to obtain a copy of my high school transcripts, but since those were in Panama—well, you get the picture.

Incidentally, these tests are administered every year across the board to all inmates. If you tank your test or refuse to take it on the grounds you already did, they give you a disciplinary write-up, remove your privileges, and assign you to education. I'm not sure what is the thinking behind this practice, but to be fair answers to the test can be purchased on the yard for a reasonable price. This means a few inmates may end up with scores that don't really reflect their true abilities. So, assuming this is what's behind the practice, a lot of money is spent every year to catch the few that cheated.

Prison educators are of the opinion that only certificates and diplomas received from them have any substance or validity. Why? Because inmates lie, cheat, and are expert con artists. It's all in the proof, I guess.

The other questionable practice or belief prison educators have is that Hispanic inmates with limited English must be assigned to education ESL (English as a Second Language). Period. This means these inmates cannot earn a living and must rely on relatives to send them money for basic needs. If they were assessed restitution as part of their sentence, the prison keeps 50% of the money sent. Friends and relatives end up being punished along with the inmate for the crime committed.

The end result of this practice is that these inmates end up doing all their prison time assigned to education attempting to learn English only to be deported back to Mexico, Central or South America in the end. This practice does ensure, however, that prison educators maintain job security.

After my TABE test, I submitted an application and was called in for an interview. Once PIA received confirmation from the education department that I was good to go, I was hired by the Print Plant. This is where they make the DMV registration tags for license plates. I started out at .20 cents an hour. I would eventually work my way up to machine operator earning .45 cents an hour. The job was not hard, and you didn't get dirty, but it was not unusual to leave the place with a terrible headache because of exposure to fumes from different chemicals used to get the work done.

Approximately two and half years later, I received a letter from my appellate attorney telling me she'd reached the end of the road with my appeals, there was nothing else to be done, and she wished me good luck. Not sure what to do, but with the words "life sentence" ringing in my ears, I went to the prison law library to seek answers.

During this time, the State was dealing with the aftermath of the Rodney King beating and the 1992 Los Angeles riots that took place after the officers involved were acquitted on the charges of use of excessive force. I remember sitting in the TV room packed with mostly Black inmates, watching the news and feeling anxious about my own safety and security. Tensions ran high, but thank goodness there were no incidents with racial overtones. I kept quiet and offered no opinions on what was going on. I silently wished I could make myself invisible.

At the law library I made the acquaintance of an inmate from San Diego named Road Dog. We lived on the same yard and the same housing unit. He was a fast-talking middle-aged White guy about five feet five inches tall with a mild case of psoriasis. His manner was bombastic, and he wrung his hands constantly as he spoke. I'd seen him on the yard playing his guitar. He inspired confidence and trust, although these feelings may have been more a reflection of my desperate state of mind than reality.

I showed Road Dog the letter I'd received from my appellate attorney. He told me not to worry. He said he knew a jailhouse lawyer who could help me. The guy's name was Blondie. He would set up a meeting since the guy lived on a different yard. I thought about this for a moment. I pulled Road Dog to the side and looked him in the eyes. I told him I had a sensitive case and was worried about information from my transcripts ending up on the yard. Road Dog smiled, put his hands on my shoulder, and said, "Everyone in this pen knows who you are." He then walked me over to a huge bulletin board in the middle of the library where I saw old newspaper clippings of infamous Colony residents, including me.

That settled, I agreed to meet Blondie. He was a Mexican American cat with a Karl Malden nose and craters on his cheeks. He had all the mannerisms of a dope fiend. He wore glasses that hung on the tip of his nose. He'd been in and out of the penitentiary all his life and was now doing a long stretch. I explained my situation, and he agreed to help me for a fee of $500. Every month he would give me a canteen list until the fee was covered. I turned over my trial transcripts and appellate briefs to him.

Blondie waited until he was paid off to show me the writ he'd prepared for me. In my opinion, the legal arguments were weak and the writing horrible. I was angry. At the first opportunity, I went looking for Road Dog. I showed him the writ and told him I thought the whole thing was garbage. He looked it over and proposed we meet on the yard at a later time to go over it and asked me to calm down.

Road Dog felt I had a point in terms of the writing but that the legal issues identified had merit. He said I should just re-write the whole thing, and then file it without saying anything to Blondie and avoid unnecessary trouble. He suggested I leave PIA and join him at the law library. He argued that I should learn law and take charge of my case. It was a choice between making money and fighting for...justice, freedom. I don't know. Maybe just fighting to stay alive. After much debate with myself I decided to make the change. He introduced me to the librarian and helped me get a position in the library.

Road Dog proved to be one heck of a friend and refused to let me feel sorry for myself or give up hope. He taught me how to be a convict. With him I learned about the great writ, the writ of habeas corpus. So, I took over litigation of my case. We talked law at work, and we talked law on the yard. The more I read, the more I studied, the more I realized what a daunting task I'd undertaken. Not only did I have to come up with an air-tight per se reversible issue, but I would have to overcome the inherent prejudicial bias that judges have against pro se litigants. But I had no other choice but to keep pushing. I felt my life depended on this. One of the first things I did when I started work was to take down the newspaper clippings from the bulletin board.

The librarian, Karen, an Irish lady in her mid-fifties with a young Dorothy Hamill hairstyle, also became very supportive of my pursuit. However, when I first met her, I didn't think she had a heart. She came across as pedantic and curt. She was a stickler for rules, which in the opinion of the workers made her more dangerous than the guards. But my purpose was to have as much access to the law library as possible, so I paid that no mind.

This much is true, it takes practice before you learn how to frame your issues properly and constitutionally. At the time of my incarceration and with the number of prisoners growing exponentially, particularly those on death row, Congress sought to limit the number of times a prisoner could use the writ to stop an execution. In April of 1996, President Bill Clinton signed into law The Antiterrorism and Effective Death Penalty Act (AEDPA) that gutted the power of the writ of habeas corpus and made it easier for states to carry out death sentences. He sacrificed prisoners' rights for political gain and essentially gave prisoners one chance to get their issues right. A second chance only if they could first prove they could touch the moon with their hands. I was happy when he was elected in 1992, but because of this law I prayed he would be impeached during the 1998 proceedings. The bastard was getting his dick sucked in the Oval Office while prisoners were living like animals in a cage. I still can't believe he survived or that Hillary did not divorce him, but that's another story. What this meant for me was that going forward to get my issues before a federal judge I would have to overcome the requirements of the AEDPA.

Road Dog was there for me with another thorn in my side.

Anticipating prison time was inevitable, I'd asked my mom to take custody of my son. She said she couldn't—that her days of raising children were over. I tear up every time I think about this. I love my mom, and I try hard not to let this development affect our relationship. However, I don't think she understood what her decision meant to me. This was a devastating blow with unending ramifications. It basically meant another consequence of my criminal conduct would be losing my son. Ironic, since it was because of him that I went ahead and married Andrea. In trying to make a right, I'd end up doing a whole lot of wrong.

He's a grown man now with children. I've not seen him since that last visit at Soledad. He used to communicate with my mom sporadically into his teens, but for many years now he has kept to himself. In case you are wondering why I don't reach out to him now…I can't. The law considers him a "next of kin" of the victim, and I'm forbidden from making contact with any next of kin or suffer the consequences. Of course, if he chose to call, write, or visit he could do so as long as he provides a notarized written declaration of his intentions beforehand. He has chosen not to do so. But I'm getting ahead of myself.

After learning of my mom's decision, I met with my ex-mother-in-law to discuss my son's future. She had been busy meeting with lawyers and social workers, determined to take custody of my son. She was like a wild animal on a mission. As you can imagine, it was not easy to have a conversation with her. The hate and contempt in her eyes were palpable. She knew Andrea had life insurance and other benefits from her employment with the county. Officials and representatives were talking to her about all this as if I was dead. She needed legal custody of my son to make things easier and to destroy any possibility of the boy maintaining any emotional connection with me.

I understood her intentions and did not think for a moment I would get understanding and cooperation from her as a father. Nevertheless, during our meeting I urged her to abandon all the legal assaults and to work with me for the sake of the boy. I told her I would leave instructions for her to take custody of the child if prison was where I was heading, that I wanted the insurance money to go in an escrow account accessible only to him on his eighteenth birthday, and a promise from her not to interfere with my parental rights. She agreed to everything, but the look in her eyes said she just wanted to take a sledgehammer to my head and pounce on me until I became gravel.

In prison, I would dial her number in an attempt to speak to my son, but she would not accept the collect calls. Desperate, I asked my mom to call her and intercede on my behalf. My mom did, and she ran into a hurricane. My ex-mother-in-law unleashed the total compliment of an artillery unit on her. Her fury came through the airwaves like a California wildfire. My mom told me she had to hang up on her because the verbal assault, laden with foul epithets, was out of this world.

I told Road Dog about my plight. He told me we needed to fight the situation in court. Together we went to work on figuring out what had to be done. I filed my petition in Family Court. It was a rudimentary petition, but since I was acting pro se the petition was accepted and my ex-mother-in-law was ordered to appear in court. She showed up with her lawyer. I represented myself via telephone as ordered by the court. This was no Atticus Finch in *To Kill a Mockingbird* performance. All I did was explain to the judge in plain English that I wanted to have a relationship with my son and communicate with him without interference. Objections were raised and my character vilified. However, in the end, the judge ruled that my parental rights had not been terminated by virtue of my incarceration, and guidelines were created so I could write and call, and the doors were open for my son to visit with me. My letters were supposed to be read to him and kept simple with loving messages. Phone calls would be arranged, but I would have to pay for them. The court order was sent to all parties that needed to know, and full cooperation and understanding was requested. Road Dog and I were totally jazzed about the outcome.

Letters were written and answered with alacrity, and telephone calls were made under strict supervision. It was not ideal, but it was something.

In the summer of 1993, I applied for and was approved for a family visit with my son and my mom. My mom travelled from Philadelphia to San Diego to pick up my son and brought him to me. We spent a weekend in a family visiting trailer. He was seven years old. My mom advised me against discussing the crime with him and encouraged me to allow him to choose the topics of conversation. The visit was without incident. He never asked what happened. For a fraction of a second, we were a family. Inside that trailer we created our own slice of paradise and acted as if all was well with the world. We ate, laughed, played, and prayed. When they left, we cried and promised to stay in touch. I had no reason to believe that our relationship would not grow stronger.

But not so fast, Kemosabe. Something happened on the way to the Forum. Things did not progress as I thought they would. Correspondence started to drag, and I began to wonder if my letters were actually given to my son. As for the phone calls…well, whenever I called, I had to endure a litany of recriminations and tearful pleas to leave them alone. Most of my fifteen minutes would be taken up by this relentless attack. I would listen for a minute, and then patiently remind her that I just wanted to talk to my son—to please hand the phone to him. She would call his name, pause, and then tell me the boy did not want to talk to me. This went on and on with no relief in sight.

Meanwhile, just when the relationship with Karen the librarian had grown comfortable, I showed up at the library to discover she'd quit. Her replacement met briefly with me to indicate it was business as usual and, no, she didn't know what happened. I went to my work area and sat at my desk trying to make sense of it all. After a moment I opened the desk's center drawer, and inside my work folder I found a letter with Karen's handwriting.

In the letter she apologized for the sudden departure and the lack of warning. She said that despite her best efforts she had developed feelings for me and was afraid if she stuck around, she would end up doing something foolish that would get us both in trouble. She left her address and phone number and asked me to get in touch if I didn't find her ridiculous.

I gave the matter some thought and decided to call her. I stupidly kept the letter. On the phone she turned out to be a different Karen. She had a home in Morro Bay and lived with her cat of whom she spoke as if she was a living person. We started corresponding, and her letters made me feel like I was Porfirio Rubirosa. This was not something I should've been entertaining, but arguments against it were forcibly dealt with like demonstrators at Tiananmen Square by the devil on my left shoulder. I sent her a visiting form application. When she returned it to the institution, all hell broke loose.

I was taken into custody by the security squad and subjected to a lengthy interrogation. The truth did not sit well with them. They speculated that I had used my convict wit to seduce and take advantage of this vulnerable female employee and they wanted me to confess. They believed I'd managed to fuck her while we were both in the library and wanted to know times and places. The library usually closed at 3:30 p.m., and we had about a half hour to clean up. With inmates getting off work and rushing to their housing units, it was busy times for the Plaza guards. They speculated this was when Karen and I would slip behind the stack of law books and I would pull her panties down and go *Escape at Dannemora* on her. I wanted to laugh in their faces, but I knew they were serious and didn't want to be roughed up. I also knew they had the power to put me in the hole and leave me there for a while.

As it turned out, the letter she'd left me when she quit and which I should've destroyed saved me. They'd searched my cell and found it. Nevertheless, they denied the visiting application just because and said she could reapply after a year. She did. And we became permanent fixtures in the visiting room.

The visits were cool and offered a respite from ordinary prison life. But I hated having to spread my ass and cough for the guards prior to returning to the yard. Something about that whole deal made me feel less than human. One of those things that make prison…well, prison. It became less bothersome on the days when Karen would give me a hand job and I would spill my seed on my underwear. It tickled me watching the guard handle the underwear full of come.

They had the last laugh, though. They took me to classification and put me up for transfer to a dorm facility. I would be sent to a place where anyone wishing to do harm would have easy access, especially at night while I slept.

The last significant thing I remember from my first tour at the Colony was sitting in the TV room on June 17, 1994, watching the LAPD chase O. J. Simpson's Ford Bronco for over an hour. Soon thereafter I'd be transferred from San Luis Obispo to Level II Avenal.

I arrived there early in 1995 and found that the staff were not inclined to grant me any special privileges. I would have to go back to court to get results. To make matters worse, I caught Valley Fever at Avenal and came close to dying. Whatever little communication I had going suffered tremendously. I did a few months at Avenal, all the while complaining that the dorm setting exposed me to much unneeded danger and requesting a transfer to a facility with cells. Someone finally took pity on me, and I was sent to Soledad Prison late in 1995. I got off the bus there right around the time O. J. was declared "not guilty" in the murder trial of Nicole.

Karen continued to visit regularly and offer moral and emotional support.

On the bus to Soledad I met some Cuban brothers who'd been there before. They gave me the layout of the place and more or less what to expect. We were kept in isolation pending classification. When we were allowed yard time, I rolled with them and was welcomed at their table. The brothers at the table told me about another Panamanian on the yard and promised to send word to him that I was awaiting classification. His name was Jose. When I met him, I sensed he was someone I could count on. He'd been in the Army, was built like a full-back, and sported a gold tooth. He was a deacon in the Protestant chapel and well-liked and respected by every community on the yard. He took time to walk around with me and introduce me to all the shot callers. We became fast friends and established a relationship that survives to this day.

14

The first thing I did when I got to Soledad was take a chance and call my son collect. I wasn't sure if the call would be accepted. To my surprise it was. I was able to speak to him. The conversation was short and sweet. The relationship with my ex-mother-in-law seemed to stabilize. Communication continued in a cordial way. Plans were made for my mom to bring my son to Soledad for a visit, and then take him with her to Philadelphia for a summer vacation. In June of 1996 I joined the California State Poetry Society and tried my hand at writing poetry. I was awful, but had fun trying.

The boy that showed up at Soledad was a bit different than the one I saw in San Luis Obispo. He was more reserved and showed less affection, taciturn. But I was delighted to see him and tried my best to make the visit a pleasant one. Something was off, but it was hard to tell what was on his mind. After leaving Soledad they travelled to Philadelphia where he spent the summer of 1996 with my mom. In Philadelphia his behavior became so erratic that my mom felt a need to document what she witnessed. Upon his return to San Diego everything changed.

It became difficult to talk to him on the phone. I made several attempts with negative results. My mom experienced the same difficulty. Finally, feeling frustrated and full of suspicions I got into it with my ex-mother-in-law. I asked her to explain the sudden change in the boy's attitude. She informed me that the boy was undergoing psychological treatment. He was acting out a lot in school and having difficulty sleeping.

I didn't know what to say. I asked if I could speak to him for a few minutes. She said he did not want to talk to me and repeated her previous pleas that I leave them alone. I remember that day well. There were lots of inmates waiting to use the phone, and of course the conversation was being monitored by the tower officer. I was lost for words. I felt defeated. I wondered what to do. I didn't want to argue, and I didn't want to do more harm. When I spoke, I just said "okay" and hung up the phone. My feet began to move, but my mind was blank. I was hurting so bad I would have welcomed a shank in my heart so that I could rest. Things had been going so well, and now it was over. I sat at an open bench, stared into space, and remembered the line in the Robert Frost poem. Absent divine intervention I still had "*miles to go before I sleep*."

Jose was there for me and encouraged me to keep the faith.

While this was happening, I still had a couple of writs in state courts, but by the time I was ready to take my issues to federal court I ran right into the AEDPA as anticipated. It takes forever for prisoner's petitions to navigate through the various state and federal courts. Only presidents, governors, attorney generals, and district attorneys get fast action. Waiting for decisions on my various petitions ate up a lot of time. What happened while waiting? Well, I'll spare the reader any account of prison horror stories, such as stabbings, suicides, riots, segregation, mutual combat, and the likes that filled the time. These things are part of daily life in prison, just the norm. Plenty has been written about that, and movies have been made on these subjects. You may remember the reports that came out in August of 1996 of fights being staged by guards at Corcoran State Prison. Rival gang members were pitted against each other, while staff betted big money on the outcome of the fights. Many inmates were shot and killed for sport. An article or two covered the scandal, but people were more interested in what was going on at the Olympics in Atlanta with Richard Jewell and the terrorist threat.

I did my best to stay clear of trouble and stuck to my plan to disappear in the Hispanic culture. I'd also started the process of continuing my law studies and just needed to iron out the logistics. Karen offered to pay for it. This is how I spent the first eight or nine years of prison time. Preoccupied with law and trying to maintain contact with my son. Domestic violence and abuse were only words I'd heard at my trial, not something I needed to work on. I did zero work on self-examination. I didn't even think I had a problem. I avoided thinking about the fatal day…night. Somehow it still felt like it had just happened.

Besides catching Valley Fever at Avenal I'd managed to stay relatively healthy, a true blessing. However, I'd been noticing a growth developing in both my eyes that was becoming more pronounced and causing irritation. I went to the library to see what I could learn about the condition. I found out it was something called pterygium, and it could affect my vision. Surgery was the only way to remove it. I put in a request to see the doctor. About a week later I received a ducat with the time and date of my appointment.

A medical appointment in prison means you're going to be at the clinic all day. You check in and are put in a cage until the doctor is ready to see you. It's standing room only, and there is no ventilation. You're never sure when you'll get to see the doctor. If you don't see him before lunch, hopefully you brought something to eat. Nothing happens while he or she is eating. And then when you do see him, the appointment is over in a few minutes. They spend more time writing notes than they do talking to you. If you're dealing with a female doctor, you have to be especially careful because they get paranoid and any accidental contact can cause them to activate their personal alarm system. That means the guards will come running ready to abuse and mistreat you.

When I spoke to the doctor about my problem, he had me sit on the examination table to take a look. He used his flashlight. I'm sure he saw the condition was bad. Nevertheless, he determined that surgery was not necessary and eye drops would do the trick. They didn't.

A couple of months later I put in another request and repeated my desire to have the growth removed by surgery. I received the same response. Ordinarily, in these situations the attending physician makes a recommendation to a panel, which then decides if surgery is warranted. I couldn't even get my doctor to agree to do that. He left me no choice but to file an appeal.

In prison an appeal is known as a 602 and it goes through various stages. First, it goes to the person you're having the problem with for an informal response. If he denies the appeal, which usually happens, the next step is to seek a formal response through the office of the appeals coordinator. If that fails to produce the relief sought, then you take it to Sacramento. After your administrative remedies are deemed exhausted, you can go to court and ask for judicial intervention.

The 602 process is arbitrary and capricious and not binding on anyone. Prison officials love to tell you your appeal was "partially granted," a hollow victory because in reality nothing changes. Decisions do not set precedent, meaning if I win an argument, another inmate with a similar situation cannot use my victory to argue his case and seek the same result. And, if the official granting the appeal vacates his position, his replacement is not obligated to honor whatever compromise was reached. All you can do is start the process all over again. Courts will not address an issue that can be resolved administratively unless you've given all parties in the chain of command a chance to do so. As you can imagine, this eats up a lot of time before you get anywhere close to a possible resolution of your complaint.

I went to war with the medical department about my eye surgery. The case went all the way to Sacramento, and I prevailed. Surgery was ordered. Since the facility was not equipped to perform that kind of surgery, I would have to be taken to an outside doctor. I was excited when I found out I would be seen by a doctor in Monterey. I figured there couldn't be any bad doctors practicing medicine in that area. And I was probably right, but they will only do work commensurate with pay.

I was placed in chains, handcuffs, and leg restraints and paraded through beautiful Monterey. People would see me coming, and they would react as if they'd seen Hannibal Lecter. The doctor himself was pleasant enough and made me feel like he would take care of me. After several visits, surgery was scheduled. Instead of using laser technology to remove the growth he just scraped the stuff off while I was under. I returned to the pen half blind. I could not walk on my own. The pain and discomfort I felt after the anesthesia wore off were out of this world. When the guards turned me over to the medical staff, they wanted to discharge me and send me back to my cell. To their credit the transportation officers said they didn't think that was a good idea. The physician on duty countered he had no beds available. A correctional sergeant had to intercede on my behalf, and make it clear to the doctor that I was not leaving the clinic in my present condition.

They found me a bed after a while, and I stayed there for five days heavily medicated and unable to open my eyes. Once I was discharged, they gave me a pair of dark glasses to wear at all times. This cause me to get stopped by every officer I came across and have to produce the note explaining medical necessity. The pterygium stayed away for a long time, but now it's starting to come back.

With so much going on and in order to keep from going crazy, I joined forces with other writ writers helping inmates appeal Board decisions, which up to that point were all arbitrary and capricious in my estimation. I started attending self-help groups and became active with the MAC (Men's Advisory Council). A neat thing I did for the MAC was start a broadcast news in partnership with the Education Department. Basically, I was videotaped reading bits of information and announcements affecting the population, and then the tape would play via closed circuit TV. It was a great experience, and it allowed me the opportunity to work closely with the Director of Education. When I received word from my law school that all I needed was a prison official to act as my proctor, I approached him and asked if he would mind acting in that capacity. He readily agreed. I started August of 1996. The partnership resulted in my receiving my law degree (Juris Doctor) from Northwestern California University School of Law on September 16, 1999. No doubt, the highlight of my prison life. Dr. Hedlund was a good man. He looked like Terry Bradshaw's twin. He was a pilot and an avid flyer. Shortly after he retired, he died doing what he loved to do.

In 1997, everyone was talking about Tiger Woods' spectacular victory at The Masters, Michael Jordan won his fifth title with the Bulls, and the people's princess, Princess Diana, left us in August. She died in a car crash in Paris, and news coverage was around the clock. Closer to home, I married Karen in the Soledad visiting room with Jose as my best man. She argued that she would be able to better advocate for me as a wife than as a friend. Maybe she wanted something in return for paying for law school. It made no difference to me since I was not allowed trailer visits anyway. I think she made the decision with her heart and without considering the ramifications. Her oldest daughter, my age, showed up. The other one didn't. There was no honeymoon. A couple of months into the marriage she grew buyer's remorse. The person who did her taxes filled her head with all kinds of doomsday scenarios, and she freaked out. I could tell that her concerns were real, so I told her to find a solution and I would support it. She decided she didn't want to be married after all. She told me not to worry, she would continue to pay for law school. I was cool with that even though law school was kicking my ass. In spite of that fact, I remained undeterred and focused. It was just me and my law books. There was no one to ask for help in explaining things I didn't understand.

In 1998, Americans became intimately familiar with Monica Lewinsky and the FDA approved Viagra. It was also the year the brief legal union to Karen ended.

And so, before I knew it, I received notice of the date of my first parole consideration hearing. My attention then shifted to this momentous occasion. I found out that there was a lot to do to prepare for such a hearing. You need letters of support, a parole plan that includes offers of guaranteed employment and a place to live, and evidence of positive programming just for a start. You also need to show remorse and accept responsibility for your crime as well as to be able to articulate and explain understanding of the underlying cause of your commitment offense. Of course, prison staff is not there to tell you this or to help you prepare. They're concerned with enforcing rules and making sure you don't escape. You mostly rely on the experience of other felons and your attorney—if you can afford to hire a good one.

When I began attending hearings, one governor famously said that the only way "lifers" would leave prison would be in a pine box. Parole hearings are very much kangaroo courts. You have the right to receive notice of the date and time of the hearing, to legal representation, and to a copy of the decision made by the panel. You're no longer innocent until proven guilty. You're now guilty as sin and a scumbag. This means that everyone present at the hearing is free to be as mean and vicious as they want to be and to tell you what you were thinking and what you actually did do on the day of the crime even though you may be the only surviving witness. Don't bother to disagree, deny, or correct, as this will just add more years to your sentence. If you can remove yourself from the equation, it is fascinating drama. However, when you are the subject of this viciousness it is actually quite traumatic.

My first experience with the Board of Parole Hearings took place on December 14, 1999, and it stunted my ability to engage in self-reflection and seek help for my emotional and psychological issues even further. I thought they'd be impressed with my efforts to obtain my law degree, but they weren't. I was given a three-year denial. I left the hearing angry and feeling very much like a victim. This took me deeper into putting my hopes for release in the judicial system. I was going to use my newly acquired JD (Juris Doctor) to properly litigate this new set of issues. I was delusional. I was also worried about Y2K. Remember that?

One of the things that made me real angry during the hearing was being mocked by the commissioners for saying that I loved my wife. But some of the inconsistencies they pointed out with that statement would later serve as the starting point for meaningful change. They stated I lacked empathy.

Up to now, I've related how events unfolded leading to tragedy but said nothing regarding my feelings towards my wife during the relationship and after her death. This is a subject that causes me a great deal of emotional turmoil.

After I made bail, I actually went to the cemetery alone to pay my respects and continued to visit the gravesite from time to time leading up to my first trial. I'm sure the visits were the product of trying to expiate guilt. But after a while it became too much to handle, and the ensuing bad dreams caused me to stop.

In the days and months that followed, I remember telling anyone who would listen how much I loved her and it was this great love that caused me to get angry with her when she drank. But when I look at how society defines love and compare it with what our relationship was from beginning to end, I come up short in every category. I was probably more concerned with how what she did or didn't do reflected on me—what did it say about me regarding the choice I'd made.

Some possible definitions of love include: "A willingness to prioritize another's well-being or happiness above your own. Extreme feelings of attachment, affection, and need. Dramatic, sudden feelings of attraction and respect. A fleeting emotion of care, affection, and like." Was any of this present in my relationship? I don't think so. There was physical attraction initially, but then even that was not enough to bridge the gap in communication and intimacy, and there was certainly no respect. Something I demanded for myself categorically.

How about what the apostle Paul said of love? "Love—agape—is patient and kind; love is not envious or boastful or arrogant or rude. It does not insist on its own way; it is not irritable or resentful; it does not rejoice in wrongdoing but rejoices in truth…love never ends" (1 Cor. 13:4-8a). No, my behavior definitely did not exemplify any of these characteristics, either. Strike two!

And how about this one? "Love is a close bond with another that goes deeper than affection, attraction, lust, or friendship. It's a deep mutual expression of respect, trust, honesty, integrity, intimacy, chemistry, and partnership. Love is something best experienced together. You find it in each other, not separately." I cannot say I recognized these feelings, emotions, or attitudes in anything I remember.

This hearing caused me to sit down and analyze what was really in my heart. To my dismay I concluded that I didn't have the faintest idea of what love was. That prompted me to ask myself then what was it that I felt for my wife, if anything, during the time we were together. I've found this difficult to articulate. I know I felt something, but that something does not come close to any of the above definitions. I often seek answers in the feelings I experienced at the hospital during the birth of my son. I know we had an emotional connection then, a bonding of sorts, but it didn't last.

She died, and I couldn't tell you any of her likes or dislikes. No favorite movie, book, actor, music, song, color, designer, sport. I didn't know if she paid attention to politics and, if so, was she liberal or conservative in her thinking. We just never talked, listened, or shared our fears and concerns. I knew she never had a relationship with her biological father. We had that in common. I knew she loved law enforcement. She never spoke about her siblings, and the relationship with her mom was complicated although the marriage and our child brought them closer to each other.

Going to Lamaze classes together and buying stuff for the baby felt good. But most of the memories I have are negative ones. Before the marriage, the Catholic classes we attended were a chore, a prerequisite. They came at the end of long days for both of us, and no effort was made to embrace the principles. Putting together the wedding production—now that's where eyes were wide open. Me—trying to hold on to my money; she—hoping to make a splash.

Today, all I'm left with is a deep sense of sadness and an inability to forgive myself for what I did. The wound has healed, but the scar remains visible for me to see every time I look in the mirror. I suppose the pain will only end when death takes me away. No amount of therapy or education can remedy that.

15

From the time I received notice of my first hearing, all conversa-tions I had started and ended with matters of parole. This may sound crazy, but not really. I hung out with nothing but lifers, so for us there was no better topic of conversation. I went to bed thinking about the Board and woke up talking about the Board—the latest court decisions, new laws, what was said in some group, what happened with a certain individual, what lawyers were having success, et cetera. Karen was good at sending any cases she thought may shed light on the current state of affairs. She was an idealist and was convinced that my prison record and good behavior would result in early release. But the more she learned about what was really going on, the more doubt started to creep into her thinking.

My next hearing took place on December 6, 2002. This is what the presiding commissioner said in his decision at this hearing:

"In the matter of Pablo Agrio, Mr. Agrio, the Panel has reviewed information received from the public and relied on the following circumstances in concluding that you're not suitable for parole and would pose an unreasonable risk of danger to society. The offense was carried out in a violent and brutal manner. These conclusions were drawn from the Statement of Fact wherein the inmate and his wife were involved in a verbal argument that became physical. A gun was introduced into the argument. There was wrestling over the weapon, at which time the inmate shot and killed his wife, causing her death. The bullet struck [the victim] in the back of the head on the neckline and travelled upwards into her skull. Inmate has no prior criminal history. During his incarceration he has received only one 128(a) counseling chrono and that was in 1991. Psychological evaluation that was dated 5/29/99, although positive, does not totally support release, in that the doctor, under assessment of dangerousness indicates that the inmate has had a very good record while in the controlled setting of the prison, but expects that he would maintain that degree of control if released to the community. He is not normally a violent person, nor does he seem to have an anger problem. He has studied the law a great deal and is a person who was able to think through a situation in a constructive manner. It also talks about the inmate being fully oriented and normal intellectual functioning. His attention and concentration was good. His insight and judgment also appear to be sound. And it doesn't indicate in his report anyplace that we're able to find that predicts any sort of threat to the community if released based upon either of the inmates in the institution or the public itself.

"The inmate does have parole plans, realistic parole plans, and does have job offers in the last county of legal residence, San Diego, and also in San Luis Obispo. Hearing Panel notes that responses to 3042 notices indicate opposition to a finding of suitability, specifically, the District Attorney of San Diego County who appeared by teleconference to oppose the inmate's release, and also the San Diego Police Department. The Panel makes the following findings. That the inmate needs additional time in order to fully understand and deal with the causation factors that led to the commitment of the life crime. Nevertheless, he should be commended.

During his incarceration he has received a law degree, been involved in AA and NA, he has been involved in the computer repair program, Arts in Corrections. He's gone through the Impact Program. He has been involved in anger management. Also, completed the business applications program. However, these positive aspects of his behavior do not outweigh the factors of unsuitability. Mr. Agrio, we denied you for a period of one year. We expect you to remain disciplinary free. If available, participate in self-help and therapy programming, and to cooperate with clinicians in the completion of a new clinical evaluation. We'll be seeking a new evaluation to answer some questions that we have.

"I'm going to speak real frank with you. As you are probably aware, we have what is called the matrix. And when we look at the matrix, you have time to serve, period. Understand that? No matter what we do today you'd have more time to serve. You've done an outstanding job as far as self-help and therapy programming while in custody. There is a question in regards to your temper. That may be explained away one way or another, but what happened that day that you shot your wife, obviously, would indicate to me that there is some sort of problem.

"Mr. Agrio, I additionally would encourage you to not let this denial be reason for you to be any different than you've been for the last…since you've been incarcerated. You have programmed tremendously, and you need to continue to do that. Good luck to you."

It seems to me that the bottom line here was that in spite of the fact that I was eligible for parole from a prison programming standpoint it had been arbitrarily decided that I hadn't been in prison long enough. Also, temper and anger management were mentioned but nothing about domestic violence, mind you. Karen was now in her mid-sixties and tired of working. She wanted to leave California and move to Hawaii.

At the May 2004 hearing, the presiding commissioner said the following:

"Okay, Mr. Agrio, the Panel have a decision. Everyone that was previously here have returned. The Panel reviewed all the information received from the public and relied on the following circumstances in concluding that the prisoner is not suitable for parole and would pose an unreasonable risk of danger to society or a threat to public safety if released from prison. One, the offense was carried out in an especially coldhearted or cruel manner. The offense was carried out in a dispassionate manner. The motive for the crime was inexplicable. The conclusion was drawn from the Statement of Facts wherein the prisoner's wife was shot by the prisoner during a domestic argument. She died of a single gunshot wound to the back of the head. The prisoner has no prior criminal history, no contact with law enforcement agencies. Under social history, it appears that up until the time of the crime, the prisoner had a stable social history, served honorably in the United States Marine Corps for seven years, a member of San Diego Police Department. It appears that he was very well connected and very well involved in that department in terms of community related programs so he's a very outstanding citizen, I'm trying to say. Certainly the Panel feels that the prisoner should continue to involve himself in self-help programs. A recent psychological report shows that the prisoner is making progress, shows that his level of dangerousness…the most recent report was in 2003, and in that report it shows that he's on the right track, shows that his level of dangerousness in a structured environment is certainly reduced. And also it shows that his level of dangerousness in an unstructured environment such as in the community is certainly reduced and it shows that he's matured and he has a good chance of being able to function in society. The prisoner does have parole plans.

"The Hearing Panel notes in response to Penal Code 3042 notices, the Deputy District Attorney from San Diego spoke in opposition. The Panel makes the following findings: The Panel finds that the prisoner should continue to involve himself in positive programs, especially self-help programs, anger management, self-control, those kinds of programs. Until enough progress is made, there is still some concern about the prisoner being an unpredictable threat to others or society. However, there are just an array of things we want to commend him for, not the least of which is he completed his education while he was in here, we're talking about a doctorate degree in law. He's been disciplinary free, he's participated in programs, Laubach tutoring programs where he helped tutor inmates both in Spanish and in English, and we certainly feel that those are significant achievements. However, at this point, those achievements do not outweigh the factors of unsuitability. Parole is going to be denied for one year. Certainly the crime has something to do with that, the manner in which the crime was carried out. We certainly recommend that he continue to participate in self-help programs with an emphasis on anger management, self-control, and if at all possible certainly domestic violence, interpersonal relationships. That concludes the reading of the decision."

At the December 2005 hearing the presiding commissioner said the following:

"Okay. This is the case of Mr. Agrio, and the time is 4:12 in the afternoon. We are reconvened. Now the panel's reviewed all the documents… all the information received from the public and relied on the follow circumstances in concluding that the prisoner is not suitable for parole and would pose an unreasonable risk of danger to society or threat to public safety if released from prison. We're going to deny your parole for three years, sir, and I'm going to tell you why. The offense in this case was particularly cruel and callous. Absolutely no motive. There was no reason for this offense to have ever occurred. It was certainly carried out in a dispassionate manner. I wouldn't go as far as to say it's an execution-style, sir. I would certainly say it's more than an unintentional act or more than an accidental death given your…given your history as a police officer, given your history as a Marine around firearms. I just find…I do not understand how this could have happened. If there wasn't…without retrying the case at all, you are here for Second-Degree Murder. I think there was certainly a crime of passion. We think it's a crime of passion. Your wife was shot to death by you over an incident that should have never escalated to clearly over that point. Along with those lines we were really wrestling with some of the things…

ATTORNEY: Excuse me, Commissioner, Mr. Agrio would like to leave the room and I will conclude the reading with just me present.

PRESIDING COMMISSIONER: Okay. Good luck to you, Mr. Agrio. Several issues as to why we determined three years. We were really wrestling with his minimalization [sic] in this first of all. He appears to be attempting to wordsmith this crime by changes in his description of this from accidental to unintentional act. Those are very far apart. His version of this changing the words from angry and infuriated, downsizing those words for the lack of better terms to upset…referring to them as upset, which makes it look a little better, a little nicer. Agrio, he said some things here that are just totally not taking responsibility. He may have mishandled the situational stress of being married to a wife who had a drinking problem and would not listen to attempts to talk. She would not listen to his attempts to talk to her in a mature manner. He's making it her fault. He's putting the monkey on her back. And I think there's something to say about the fact that he didn't want to hear the truth here and didn't want to face the facts and left the hearing prematurely. The reason…one of the reasons that people in law enforcement and people with experience with domestic violence know it happens all the time, and that is when a woman is battered, police are called, she calls them as the right thing to do, and then as soon as things settle down, then she recants, and that's what appears to have happened here. When the internal investigation was taking place, she backed off because she's going to lose. If he loses his job or gets suspended, then she's going to lose. If he gets convicted of battery, then she's going to lose, and so I mean this is typical where the spouse backs off.

I think he was, the most honest I think he was to us here today or to the system was the statement he made when he analyzed the cultural terms of a Latin family where a man is the boss of the house and ordinarily the wife jumps at the snap of a finger. He indicates that today's younger people are not traditionalist in an attempt to explain his position. I think he's right on. I think he's right on, and if you study cultures you know that some cultures, a lot of cultures have their cultural things. Sometimes in different cultures you have to break those. From those…those are the reasons that we…that we're giving him for this multiple-year, three-year defile. His previous record, absolutely no jail time, no criminal conduct that we know of. However, he does have, as evidenced in more than one place, a record of violence or assaultive behavior leading up to this incident. His institutional behavior he's had one 128A. He should be commended for his institutional behavior no 115. He knows how to operate within an institution. He was a good Marine. He was a good policeman, and he's being a model prisoner, and I think that he responds well to institutionalization, and that 128 was in 1991 for contraband, and he gave us a reason that sounded pretty reasonable to me. He was new on the block. There's no question that this man could be a success. The law business on the outside, the deputy commissioner brought up some ideas for him in terms of starting the process to get his bar card as to how…he gave suggestion as to how he should be pursuing that in the State of California.

"The 3042 response the San Diego County District Attorney opposes parole for Mr. Agrio, and as you read this I'm going to stop beating this up, but I want to make sure the record reflects the good things that you have done. You are a disciplinary clerk as of '04, you've done data processing. You've got satisfactory to exceptional work reports. You've obtained your law degree. You've been through the Impact course. You've been in the business course, Cage the Rage, anger management in '04 and '05, Buddhist meditation, and AA since year 2000. You've done the spiritual recovery program. You were active in the Veterans group, musical therapy prison ministry as well as a volunteer worker in the arts and hobbies area…arts and corrections, I should say. You've received numerous laudatory Cronos for your work. It appears that you have a great work ethic and that you put your heart and soul into your work and into your vocations and into your self-help projects that you have been involved in.

"In a separate finding we are going to say that you are to confront your demons in terms of the insight into the crime, your responsibility into this crime. It just didn't happen. There was…this was a crime of passion, and we would encourage you not to have such selective and minimalized [sic] memory. Again, your parole denial is three years."

After this hearing, Karen informed me that she was selling her house and moving to Hawaii. She would continue to be supportive as best she could, but she had to do what was best for her. I completely understood. The situation seemed hopeless. We had to deal with reality. No amount of wishful thinking was going to make things better.

The three-year denial hit me hard. Lifers from all races felt frustrated with the Board. I could tell by listening to the conversations on the yard. Most felt the answer was finding a court that would take the time to look at the issues being litigated seriously. And by the way, have the courage to buck the system. Some judges may have understood what was taking place but were unwilling to sacrifice their careers for a bunch of convicted killers.

An idea began to percolate in my mind. Individually, few could afford to retain a lawyer to fight their cases long term. But what if we all came together and hired an attorney to file a class action lawsuit? I spoke to Jose about what I had in mind. He was supportive right away. He expressed concern for who that lawyer would be and the cost of such an enterprise. I told him I would check with Karen about the lawyer.

I contacted the lawyer Karen referred me to, a Mr. Smith, and he agreed to visit me time permitting. When he showed up, I made my pitch and asked if he'd be willing to help. Mr. Smith said he would be interested in such an undertaking, but we would have to come up with at least $60,000 to start and sustain the lawsuit, and that depending on how far he had to go, more would probably be needed. He agreed to accept collect calls from me and correspond regarding any progress made on my end.

With Jose's assistance I started having conversations with the various lifer communities to get a feel for their views on the matter. The leaders were cool, but it was felt that a general meeting was necessary to give everyone a chance to ask questions and make up their own minds. A meeting on the yard was a problem because guards got very nervous when large groups of inmates started congregating. After much discussion it became clear the meeting would have to take place in the chapel.

To that end we met with the Muslim brothers and sought their support. They had use of the chapel in the afternoons right when most guys were getting off work. We asked them to speak to their Imam and explain what we were trying to accomplish. The leaders said it was better if I made the request and that they would facilitate an interview.

A meeting with the Imam was arranged. Jose agreed to go with me. We met in the Imam's small office surrounded by his assistants. They were standing against the wall like they were guarding a VIP. I'd seen him before but never really had an opportunity to speak to him. After the introductions and some small talk, I told him what I was trying to do. He agreed to help in exchange for five to ten minutes where he could address the group.

A date was set. I went to work on spreading the word. Some did not like the ten minutes deal, but I argued it was the best we could do.

The day of the meeting the turnout surprised us all. The chapel was packed, standing room only. I sat with the Muslim brothers by the altar behind the pulpit. The Imam had never had that kind of crowd for his service. He kept his word and spoke for about ten minutes. Guys were quiet and respectful. When he was done he nodded in my direction and walked off towards his office. No doubt he saw me in a different light then.

I spoke to the crowd confidently. I wrote down questions I couldn't answer and kept the meeting rolling. The sticking points were the honesty and credibility of Mr. Smith and the collection and accountability of funds. We agreed to keep meeting and talking until we had a plan everyone could support. The Imam agreed to let us continue to meet in the chapel provided he had advanced notice and we didn't interfere with his regular program.

After a couple more meetings and not finding a unanimous voice, doubt started to creep into my thought process. I decided to address Mr. Smith's credibility by extending an invitation to him to speak to the group directly. I knew I'd gained credibility with the Imam so arranging another meeting was not a problem. Getting him to sponsor Mr. Smith, however, would require some convincing.

It took months to get everything to fall into place. Any number of issues kept coming up. Vacations, work schedules, prison lockdowns, religious holidays, et cetera. In the meantime, I tried to convince Mr. Smith that the money thing could be settled by him agreeing to have participants send contributions directly to him. He'd keep the funds in an escrow account and provide me with a spreadsheet I could show the population. Everyone would be able to see who had donated, how much, and where we were relative to our goal. Mr. Smith didn't like the idea. He said it'd be too much hassle for him and his staff.

When he saw the crowd at the chapel, he changed his mind. He answered questions and showed enthusiasm. But the crowd went sideways on me. While before the sticking points were credibility and accountability, the crowd now wanted guarantees. And they wanted to know whose name would be on the lawsuit. Until then no one had given that much thought, but it took me just a second to guess the reason behind the question. It was assumed that my name would be front and center and any success or benefit would be on me while the rest were left behind. After all, this was all my idea and Mr. Smith was my friend.

Nevertheless, we left that meeting with a working plan. Mr. Smith gave his business address and promised to set up the escrow account. He did.

The money started to trickle in. After about two months, when I received the first report, I was terribly disappointed. We hadn't even cracked $3,000. People were sending in five, ten, twenty dollars at most. A handful had contributed fifty and a hundred. At that rate it would take years before we got near the goal. I needed to drive this point home urgently.

I went to the Imam to arrange another meeting at the chapel but ran into problems right away. The Imam wanted more than ten minutes. I gently tried to explain to him that guys would become upset if he took too long. He was determined. As I feared, after the fifteen-minute mark the White brothers walked out. Soon, others followed. By the time he was done talking I'd lost two-thirds of the chapel and those still there were mostly Black. The display felt offensive by some, and all the goodwill generated to that point was lost.

Undeterred I kept pushing, but the message was no longer being heard. No matter what I tried, contributions did not pick up. In the end we didn't even reach the $10,000 mark. No one wanted to hear anything about another meeting at the chapel. Guys started coming up to me demanding their money back. A clear signal it was over. It would take months to settle affairs with all those who contributed. What a fiasco. Mr. Smith was pissed. Some claimed they never got their money or were sent less than what they'd put in. I'd learned a valuable lesson in leadership. Nothing left to do but to get ready for the next Board hearing.

In 1997 Angela Davis, Ruth Wilson Gilmore, and Rose Braz founded an organization called *Critical Resistance*. It's a national, member-based, grassroots organization that works to build a mass movement to dismantle the prison-industrial complex. In the spring of 2005 they launched *The Abolitionist*, a bilingual publication dedicated to the strategy and practice of prison-industrial complex abolition. The paper was distributed free of charge to over 7,000 people in prisons, jails, and detention centers throughout the US, who in turn shared the paper with many more fellow prisoners.

I came across an issue left on a table in the game room, and not having anything else to do but wait for the hourly unlock, I started perusing it. Right away I was struck by the message and the reporting. The articles echoed my perception of the justice system in the state and validated my frustration. I went to work on a piece hoping it would fall on sympathetic ears and get published.

The article, *Attainder in California: Alive and Well*, was published in Issue 4 of the summer of 2006. Attainder is a common law term defined as the act of extinguishing a person's civil rights when sentenced to death or declared an outlaw for committing a felony or treason. A Bill of Attainder is a special legislative act prescribing capital punishment, without a trial, for a person guilty of a high offense such as treason or a felony. Bills of attainder are prohibited by the United States Constitution.

Although I was super excited when the article came out, I knew I was preaching to the choir. The editor's note drove the point home. It said,

"Pablo Agrio's 'Attainder in California' touches on the importance of understanding how victims' rights groups like Justice for All, Crime Victims United of California, and the Doris Tate Crime Victims Bureau effectively lobby for increasingly punitive prison terms, conditions of confinement, and 'no-parole' policies. Their support of highly emotional victim impact statements during sentencing and parole hearings remain controversial.

"Conservative victims' rights groups have close working relationships with the Justice Department, district attorneys, police, and in the case of Crime Victims United of California and the Doris Tate Crime Victims Bureau: direct financial dependence on the California Correctional Peace Officers Association (CCPOA). This translates into unchecked abuses of power and influence. For example, Crime Victims United of California were outspoken opponents of Prop 66, which would have reformed certain aspects of California's Three Strikes Law and resulted in a smaller prison population. This directly counters the interests of the CCPOA. Susan Fisher, the new chairwoman of the California's Board of Parole Hearings (previously the Board of Prison Terms), was herself formerly the director of the Doris Tate Crime Victims Bureau. The stacking of the Board of Parole Hearings with victims' rights advocates and former cops results in de facto 'unsuitability' rulings against eligible parolees. The current backlog of roughly 3200 parole hearings, coupled with denials for parole reconsideration for up to 5 years as a way to manage this caseload, directly violates California Penal Code 3041(a).

"Importantly, 'the majority of victim activists are White, middle-class, and female, which is far from representing the average victim of crime' and 'ignore victims of corporate crimes, State violence, human rights abuses, and environmental racism' (see Defending Justice, pages 204 and 205, available for free download at: http://www.defendingjustice.org/). As abolitionists it is time we figure out decarceration strategies for lifers that support reconciliation and community accountability for survivors of interpersonal violence and ensure the safety and self-determination of all members of society. Otherwise, lifers too are sentenced to a slow death behind bars."

Like everything else, the article can be found on the internet if you're curious. I was proud of what I wrote then and remain proud today. In re-reading the article I felt all the raw emotion that overcame me when

I went to work on it. I was hoping to get a reaction from someone who cared, but unfortunately as is the case when your life doesn't matter only the paper's editor and yours truly took the time to ponder the point I was making.

At the December 2008 hearing the presiding commissioner said the following:

"Ready? The time is now 24 minutes after 4. It should be noted for the record that all parties that were present prior to our recess for deliberations is back in the room, including two Correctional Peace Officers that will not be participating in this hearing, but are here for security purposes. Mr. Agrio, the Panel reviewed all information received from the public and all relevant information that was here before us today in concluding that the prisoner is not suitable for parole. He poses a present risk of danger to society or a threat to public safety if released from prison. The finding of unsuitability is based on weighing the considerations provided in the California Code of Regulations Title XV. This is a three-year denial. The first consideration which weighed very heavily towards unsuitability is the commitment offense, sir. The offense was carried out in a manner which demonstrates an exceptionally callous disregard for human suffering. On two separate occasions your wife was a victim of battery, to which the second incident of battery she was shot in the back of the head, which killed her. The motive for the crime is inexplicable. Normally, the only one left that we have to assess the story that they're telling is the person who committed the murder, because the victim cannot speak. But we have an opportunity here where one of our victim's next-of-kin's relatives, or assistant, who lived in the house, who lived in the house for six months, says she never saw any substance abuse problems with alcohol.

"And then, one thing that puzzled me, your wife went to the academy. I remember going to an academy, and I didn't have time for any drinking. I had to be up early in the morning, study late at night, and there was no time for drinking. So, sir, the Panel doesn't buy the chemical addiction that you were throwing us today. We believe the motive for the crime was control. Dominance. We've seen pictures of your wife. Your daughter, ma'am. She is a beautiful woman. She was a beautiful woman.

"Sir, you're right. You do meet a lot of suitability factors. No prior criminality. Not an unstable social history. No previous incarcerations, any juvenile history, any adult history. But what also fell heavily towards unsuitability was your past and present mental attitude towards the crime. As I spoke, sir, you blame, primarily, your wife's drinking, her chemical dependence, for what started this whole thing. And the other thought process I had, I never heard you say that you tried to get her help with any kind of rehab. And I would think that's what you would try to do if somebody had a chemical dependency, or be able to prove to the courts that you placed her in rehab to get her help. And that's why we find, one, you blame your wife for the drinking that caused the issue, and two, you're not credible because of what I stated about the witness being here that lived in your house for six months, plus the fact that your wife had graduated from the academy. And if she was drinking how could she possibly graduate from the academy?

"The prisoner lacks insight into the causative factors of his conduct, and I really, and the Panel really appreciates you coming in here and setting the record straight and telling the truth for the first time that you were responsible and accountable for your wife's murder, and it was not an accident. But, sir, you lied to the Board three previous times. So I can't understand how you feel you can come in today and have this evolution and tell the truth and expect the Panel to disregard the lie you told on three separate occasions. As I stated before the prisoner's current mental state, attitude towards the crime, I really believe, sir, you came partway across today with the honesty. I think there's more insight you need to find.

"What makes perfectly good sense is what she said here at the hearing, that the wife asked you to go to the party in front of someone else where you could not say no. You had so much control of this woman, that she had to ask another grown adult for permission to go somewhere. That's dominance, sir. My wife doesn't ask me, she tells me where she's going. You had her reporting to you like she was a child. Call it what it is. Come out and call it what it is, sir.

"You're right, other things that have factors towards your suitability, you have no 115's. You do show remorse for what happened, and you do have realistic parole plans. I've also talked to you, sir, about Penal Code Section 3042, and that's why we have the District Attorney representative here from the County of San Diego, and also the letter I read into the record from San Diego Police Department. Both oppose your parole suitability.

"You have a law degree, you have a paralegal degree, you have numerous Chronos from different staff in support, you had a lot of different self-help programs, you had a lack of assaultive history as a juvenile, you have a lack of a criminal history, you had somewhat of a stable social history being a Marine, and also a police officer. And your age, your present age, reduces recidivism risk because you're now 50 years old, plus the fact that you've had no serious misconducts for 20 years.

"While the Panel wants to commend you for the positives, on the balance the circumstances that make you unsuitable for parole, which we have already discussed with you, heavily outweigh the positive aspects of your case. After weighing all the evidence presented today, you are unsuitable for parole because you remain a present risk of danger if released, and require at least an additional three years of incarceration. Please, sir, read the transcript, please. I'm going to tell you, one day you're going to get out of here. I know people don't want to hear it, but I'm just going to be factual with you. You've started today by telling the truth. You're doing the work inside the prison, but your insight has to be able where everyone can draw the conclusion that you get it, and you're ready to leave. You also have to remember, sir, regardless if the Panel finds you suitable, it still goes in front of the Governor and the Governor's staff will review. It does not make sense if you cannot get past that to send you there. Do you understand? So, get right, keep working, and work your way out. Okay?"

In November of 2008 Senator Barack Obama became the first African American elected president of the United States. The U.S. boasted 1,610,446 prisoners in both state and federal jurisdictions. Data showed 1 in every 198 persons in the U.S. resident population was incarcerated. In California alone there were 173,320 inmates scattered around 33 prison institutions. There was a rumor going around that the state had built more prisons than colleges and universities dating back to 1965. The California Correctional Peace Officer Association (CCPOA) was considered the most powerful political force in California politics.

16

The December 2008 three-year denial was reduced to two years on appeal, which meant I returned for a new hearing in November 2010. By then I had been transferred from Soledad Prison back to San Luis Obispo. That hearing resulted in another three-year denial.

To date then, I had amassed a grand total of fourteen years' worth of denials despite my best efforts to rehabilitate myself. I would go through stages of deep depression and feelings of hopelessness only to bounce back by thinking that maybe there was something else I needed to do or could do that would make the difference at the next hearing. It was absolute madness. I worked my prison job, and when I was done with that, I worked on parole issues. I found inspiration in people like Nelson Mandela, Aung San Suu Kyi, Jawaharlal Nehru, Vaclav Havel, Malcolm X, Elie Wiesel, and some of the great Russian writers such as Aleksandr Solzhenitsyn who wrote *The Gulag Archipelago*—people who had done prison time for various reasons and had managed to emerge strong from the experience.

Some crazy thoughts entered my mind during this time. Since I was deemed a threat to this society, I considered what would happen if I offered to renounce my citizenship and asked the authorities for immediate deportation. I researched the subject and even corresponded with attorneys who claimed to know about these things. I found out that to renounce your citizenship you have to do it in person. It cannot be done by mail. You must also be in a foreign country at the time and appear before a diplomatic officer to sign an oath of renunciation. And you must prove that you have or can obtain citizenship in another country simultaneously. You cannot be stateless and lack protection from a government.

Unable to get anywhere with this thought process, I then wondered if I could request transfer to a military facility such as Fort Leavenworth. Again, this idea gained no traction and proved another dead end. These are but a couple of examples of the kinds of things that enter your mind when you feel you are on a train destination extermination camp.

I'd grown old, was weary and tired, and for the first time began considering the possibility that I'd reached the end of the road in my life. It appeared that my true punishment would be death in prison. I'd come to America in pursuit of a better life and managed instead the complete opposite. And it was all my doing. I'd become the principal architect of my own demise.

Various governors came and went; prisons became overcrowded; the number of aging inmates multiplied, and the only self-help programs available in prison were Narcotics Anonymous (NA) and Alcoholics Anonymous (AA). If you had problems with drugs and alcohol, you were good. If you had other issues, you were on your own.

As I approached my third decade of incarceration, a mild wind of change began to blow. A state court of appeals finally granted a writ filed by a lifer against the board, and in their decision gave specific instruction on the duties of the board and the governor when dealing with matters of parole. The writ was crafted by high-powered attorneys hired by the inmate's family. This gave everyone hope that things would be different going forward. But not so fast—incredibly enough, on appeal, the State Supreme Court ruled that the findings of the appellate court applied only to the inmate in question and not to anyone else. However, the federal courts were also looking at the issue of overcrowding and applying pressure on state officials to address this issue. Inmates were dying because of overcrowding.

I started my incarceration at the Men's Colony in San Luis Obispo, and after a tour at Avenal and more than ten years at Soledad, a classification committee decided I should return there. It was on the bus there when I experienced an epiphany. I was in handcuffs and leg restraints, riding the CDC bus with a bunch of old men, men no longer mean and angry looking, but men resigned to their fate, when looking out the window I decided to give up the fight. I would no longer litigate. If I was going to meet my maker from a prison cell, so be it.

I was on my way to chow one morning soon after my arrival at SLO when I saw a flyer announcing an open invitation to attend mass. I hadn't attended Catholic mass since my Marine Corps days. Without thinking too much about it, I showed up. Sitting in church I began to reflect on how I'd managed to make a mess of my life and all the pain, misery, and suffering I'd left in my trail. I became teary eyed. I determined I would continue to attend mass regularly and try to find peace of mind in the scriptures. I volunteered to serve during mass and sought counseling from the priest. I got involved with the Veterans in Prison group and started to facilitate self-help groups. I went back and read some of the things commissioners had said about me at prior parole hearings. It was hard to read. I noticed a common theme. The words "domestic violence," "abuse," "power and control," "lack of empathy," and "no remorse" were scattered all over those pages.

Coincidentally, right around this time Sacramento instituted a program known as LTOP (Long Term Offender Program) that provided cognitive behavioral treatment and other rehabilitative programs for lifers besides AA and NA. I not only voluntarily enrolled in this program but also sought individual therapy from the psychology department at the institution. In a stroke of luck, I was assigned a therapist. Ordinarily they only work with inmates who are seriously mentally ill and housed in special units.

Instead of working to secure a parole date, I started working to understand myself. This is difficult and painful work. There are so many compartments, but they are all interrelated. You open the door to one, and the stench is unbearable. The default reaction is to quickly step back and close the door. This is where a good therapist helps. On my own there would've never been any exploration. Some memories are real, some are imagined. They began almost as soon as I had use of reason. My young mind's inability to understand certain things about the adult world caused trauma. My coping mechanism was to create my own imaginary secret world, and then disappear into it. As I got older, I was introduced to the concept of violence as an acceptable way to resolve conflict. In my neighborhood, in the media, at school, in the park—violence was everywhere. No matter where I looked, rewards and punishments were the effective model.

As for domestic violence, I don't remember witnessing that in my home, but it was all around me. I came to believe that to minimize pain and suffering I had to take control of my immediate environment. If I depended on others to do well by me, they were sure to let me down.

One of the first things I discovered in therapy was my penchant for talking about my crime in terms of what my wife had done or failed to do. I had to learn to talk about what *I* did and leave my wife out of it. It was the only way to take full responsibility for my actions and behavior.

I worked hard to understand the concepts and labels that were thrown at me. I had to discard notions and beliefs I had about them and wrap my head around their application in the present world. I had to learn to listen and accept constructive criticism.

For example, prior to this experience I didn't consider name calling and put-downs as being abusive. And I didn't see my violent outbursts as abusive either, but more of a form of discipline. Sounds crazy, right? What about making unilateral decisions and managing all the money as constituting power and control? Oh no, I knew better and it was safer that way. I think you get the picture.

Well, that's why this kind of self-examination is often avoided, because what begins to emerge is the picture of a despicable person. I confess I wasn't wired to think of myself as a bad guy. On the contrary, all along I fancied myself a loving and caring husband, a decent law-abiding citizen, a good father, a good neighbor, a God-fearing man. This kind of work requires complete honesty and commitment. I had to be willing to abandon the old self and become a new man. You need help in doing this, and it cannot be done in ninety days or twelve months. Not when you're trying to undo a lifetime of emotional and psychological issues. Anger, bitterness, and resentment are not toys to be played with. Unchecked, they are a recipe for disaster.

17

On January 2011, I watched Gov. Arnold Schwarzenegger wait until his last day in office to announce the commutation of convicted killer Esteban Nunez, the son of a powerful political ally, and then give as an explanation: "Of course you help a friend." In October 2008, Nunez and his co-defendant stabbed to death Luis Santos, a 22-year-old San Diego Mesa College student. The Governor's decision reduced Nunez's sentence from 16 years to 7 years in prison. In his written explanation, the Governor said it was unfair that co-defendant Jett and Nunez should get the same sentence, considering that Nunez had no prior record, though Jett did. I couldn't help but think to myself how different my predicament would be if I too had a friend in the Governor's Office.

In April of 2011, while working with the Inmate Peer Education Program (IPEP)and at the request of the mental health department, I wrote and acted in a short suicide prevention video that was so well received by prison administrators that it was ordered played in all CDC prisons. It's probably still being played to this date. A proud moment to be sure, for all those involved.

At the October 2013 hearing the presiding commissioner said the following:

"All right. The time is about 12:50 now. And we are back on the record to…we've convened the hearing to share the Panel's decision in the matter of Mr. Pablo Agrio. All parties are back in the room now. Mr. Agrio was received by the CDCR on May 15th, 1989, from the County of San Diego, and is serving a sentence of 17 years to life for Murder in the second degree of his wife at the time. She was 23 years old at the time of her death. Now in making our decision today, Mr. Agrio, we considered all the information that we deemed relevant and reliable. And we considered the entire written record before us, the additional documents that you provided. We went through and read through the book reports, the relapse prevention plan, the additional letters. All the documents you submitted today were considered. We also considered the letters that were received from the… from the public, from the Public Defender's Office. We reviewed the confidential portion of your Central File. And we did not rely on the contents of the file because they speak largely to immutable factors. And those were all considered during…were discussed and considered as part of the total presentation. We considered your testimony today and note that your attorney spoke in support of your parole, and the District Attorney's Office spoke in opposition.

"The fundamental question that we had to answer was whether or not you pose a potential threat to public safety if you were to be released on parole. And this was a very difficult question. It's probably…the testimony of that is the length of deliberation. And we did consider all of the above factors, all the suitability factors, all the unsuitability factors, and all the pros and cons. The bottom line is we have to rely on evidence in the record of your current dangerousness. And after all is said and done, we found that Mr. Agrio does not pose an unreasonable risk of danger to society or a threat to public safety, and is therefore eligible for parole.

"Now the record does reflect factors tending to show unsuitability. But on balance, we felt that you do not pose an unreasonable risk of dangerousness today. The decision does not diminish the fact that the life crime that you committed was an absolutely horrendous act. And you couple that with the fact that you were a sworn peace officer, sworn to uphold the law. We hold peace officers at the highest standard. And for me, as a peace officer and a former...as a retired peace officer, that just made this decision extremely difficult. But that said, we arrived collectively at this decision. And I'll explain why in a minute.

"The act that you committed, basically, was the result of an intense argument between you and your wife, who was about to graduate and become a sheriff's correctional officer herself. She was to be a woman in uniform, your equal. And I think, more than anything, that really grated on you more than anything. We didn't talk about that today. But I believe that to be the case. She went out to celebrate the fact that she was about to graduate from the correctional officer academy, San Diego Sheriff's Department. And she came home late after being out drinking with her girlfriends. And as time progressed, you got angrier and angrier and angrier. And when she got home, you got into an argument with her. She just wanted to go to sleep and sleep it off. But you goaded her and goaded her. At one point, she got up and closed the door when you left. And you kicked the door in, basically. At one point during the argument, she picked up a coat, a jacket that was sitting on the bed and started to hit you with it. And you kicked her. Severe, large...left large bruises on her leg. She tried to call the police. She ran for the phone. You grabbed the phone away from her and tossed it in a drawer. Then she ran to the kitchen and tried to get that phone. You did the same thing. And then at some point, you know, at some point, she basically just felt like, well, you know what, he's probably going to kill me. That thought probably occurred to her. And at one point, the...one of her girlfriends called. And you said that you weren't done with her yet. I'm not sure exactly what you meant by that at the time. But she reached for your service revolver. You grabbed it away from her. A struggle ensued. And we had some discussion about that.

"You were found guilty of Murder in the Second Degree. You have been serving a lengthy sentence as a result. You called the police. And she was already dead by the time they got there. You had multiple opportunities to cease. And you never did. All you could think about was, you know, your…you were angry, your perfectionist nature, your controlling nature, your sexist views of women and women's role in the marriage. All of that, apparently, was part of what was driving your emotions and your anger on that day. And it ultimately led in the death of a woman that you purported to love. And you left a son an orphan.

"So we also noted that you had an unstable social history. You had really no relationship with any woman prior to your wife. Yes, you had a lot of sexual encounters. You said you had 50 to 75 casual sexual encounters with partners and prostitutes. But those hardly amount to a stable social history. You also had no relationship with your father, no relationship with your son since the life crime. So all that points to an unstable social history. Still, all that said, the California Supreme Court has directed us that after a long period of time where there has been a considerable amount of rehabilitation on the part of the inmate, that he or she has participated, genuinely participated in their own rehabilitation and has made significant strides in that direction and has had a change in their mental state toward the life crime, that the immutable factors of the commitment offense and the… and the unstable social history may no longer suggest that you still remain a threat of danger to society. And that's the question that we struggled with.

"In your case, 25 years have passed, and many of the circumstances that tend to show suitability are present. You have accepted responsibility for the life crime. At least you have verbalized that. Now that has been a change. I don't know exactly how it evolved. But at the time of your, the jury trial, you were still claiming it was an accident. We know today that that was no way on earth an accident. You were angry. You got angrier. You were controlling. You were a perfectionist. And your wife, who was drinking, somehow did not rise to that model of the perfect wife anymore. Because she was somehow flawed because she could drink. And more than anything, she was flawed because she didn't live according to whatever expectations you had of her.

"Now the fact of the matter is that today, we believe you have an understanding of what your character flaws are. And you've done a lot of treatment. And we commend you for that. Because not a lot of inmates are willing to raise their hand and say, hey, I need some therapy, I need some help. And maybe you went there because it's something that you can't speak about openly among inmates. And I understand that. But it doesn't matter how you got there. It's just important that you did. And we read some of your writing, your book reports. We read your relapse prevention plan. And to be honest with you, it was that relapse prevention plan that tilted the scale.

"Today, you described a cerebral and academic understanding of your character flaws. But in the relapse prevention plan, you've turned it more into an action item. And the problem with domestic violence cases is it's very difficult to demonstrate in prison, in a controlled environment, that you can actually carry out this plan. It's only when you get released and you're out in the free community that you can show that you've really learned something and what you've learned up here intellectually has actually become part of who you are, your nature, and all the stuff that you talked about isn't just lip service. Because I questioned that. During the hearing, I listened very carefully to your words. Because I wanted to make sure that you were not just trying to pull wool over our eyes. But I think at your core you understand that it is wrong to be controlling, it is wrong to be a bully, it is wrong to lay your hands on a woman. And it is absolutely cowardly to lay your hands on a woman and ultimately to kill her. And that's what you did. And you have had to live with that for the last 25 years. You're going to have to live with that for the rest of your life.

"And I pray that we made the right decision here, and you don't violate another woman. But part of what we relied on also was when you talked about how you learned. You had to reflect while you were in prison. And you realize, wow, it's the women in my life that have helped me change. You look to your therapist, your teachers. People who have supported you, they have all been women. And so we hope that that stays with you. That's something that, you know, just sitting there with you, and you treat women with respect and dignity and the equals that they are.

"Okay. We think that you've demonstrated your remorse through some of the living amends that you've done. You've participated in a number of charitable events. You're actively involved. Apparently, you have a passion for the Veteran's group. You want to help other veterans like yourself. You also...you also participated in the translation of an anger management program for...into Spanish for Spanish-speaking inmates. That's direly needed in prison. And I know that if you translated the program, you had to have learned something. You obviously have marketable skills. You've gotten your college degree, your JD while in prison. So all that's in good order.

"But our decision is not final. It has to be reviewed by the Decision Review Unit in Sacramento. And it has to be reviewed by the Governor's Office. If the Governor disagrees with us, which he sometimes does, then you will be informed of that change in writing. So we had to come up with your terms of confinement. And the...we had to do the term calculation. The base offense we utilized was Murder in the Second Degree. We applied the matrix 2403(c). We used column C because there was severe trauma in the murder. The death resulted in, or death came from the wound that was inflicted with the…with the weapon. Row two was applied because there was a prior relationship between you and the victim. The term was aggravated because of the weapon and the peace officer status, opportunity to cease, vulnerable victim, the special relationship that you had with her. All of those are factors that would aggravate the crime. We then applied…there were no ineligible years where you couldn't receive any credit, post-conviction credit because you had no 115's. So that was positive. There were 22 satisfactory years. There was one year in which we provided extra credits because of the academic upgrades that you did. So the bottom line is you received 96 months of post-conviction credits. So that results in a past date, which means that if the Governor agrees with us, if it gets through Decision Review, if the Governor agrees, then you would be released from prison immediately. You would have no additional time to serve. So with that, we want to wish you well, Mr. Agrio. This hearing is now adjourned. The time is 1:25."

As excited as I was for the finding of suitability, the commissioner's last words gave me an uneasy feeling. By law, the Governor had about four months to either allow the decision to stand by taking no action, actively approve the decision, modify the decision (i.e., adding a parole condition or changing a parole date), reverse the Board's decision, or refer the decision back to the Board so that all of the commissioners can reconsider the Panel's decision.

Those four months proved to be very difficult for me. For one thing, the word got around that I had been found suitable for parole and was on my way home. Not a day went by that someone wasn't congratulating me and wishing me well. I didn't want to think about the possibility, but I got caught up in the moment and started preparing to leave. I gave away all my property, including my TV and other miscellaneous stuff that makes daily prison life livable. Everything was reduced to what could fit in an average size grocery bag.

At the last minute, a guard came by my cell and gave me a pass to go pick up legal mail at the office. It was a letter from the Governor's Office. I felt sick to my stomach. I knew it was bad news. I had seen others go through the same painful experience. The letter said:

"Dear Mr. Agrio:

Article V, section 8 of the California Constitution and Penal Code section 3042.1 authorizes the Governor to review parole decisions of the Board of Parole Hearings concerning people sentenced to an undetermined term upon conviction of murder. The Governor exercised his review authority in your case, and after carefully considering the record, he decided to reverse the Board's decision to grant parole."

It was dated January 24, 2014, and signed by Governor Edmund G. Brown, Jr.

The Governor stated that he acknowledged my efforts to improve myself while incarcerated but those efforts did not outweigh the negative factors that demonstrated I remained unsuitable for parole. The listed factors were that the crime was senseless and callous, I lacked understanding of my control issues, I was not able to explain why I harbored sexist views of women, why I needed to micromanage every aspect of my wife's life and how I came to dehumanize her to the point that I could kill her. He encouraged me to comprehensively explore what about my past or personality turned me into a "killer" so that going forward I could "deal constructively with any issues that may arise in any future romantic relationships."

So it was back to the drawing board. On hearing the news some guys came by the cell and returned the property I'd given away. Others kept the stuff and thought nothing of it. I really didn't care. Even though I'd been acquitted of First-Degree Murder by a jury, I was now essentially doing time for that crime. I wondered how many guys that entered the prison system at the same time I did, with First-Degree Murder convictions, were actually paroling before me. It became clear to me that the actual application of the law meant that there was really no distinction between First- and Second-Degree murder since the punishment was entirely at the discretion of the Governor. I also wondered how many inmates had actually died in prison while subjected to discretionary authority.

It took a lot of will power to get back on my horse and keep pushing, so to speak. And things would only get worse. I didn't bother to file an appeal. I struggled to keep it together. I was like a character in The Walking Dead. And before I knew it, lo and behold, I was called back to the Board April 2015. I'd done zero preparation for this hearing. I was not sharp and actually carried with me a bit of an attitude. I was not aware of it, but it was right there under the surface. It manifested itself in sarcasm and cynicism. When the presiding commissioner asked me how I felt about what the Governor had done, my tongue ran away from me. I asked why the Governor had a Board if he didn't trust their judgment. I wanted to know if he actually reviewed my case personally or if someone else had made the decision for him and just had him sign off on it. I questioned what he wrote and how he came to his decision if he'd never met me. I was off the charts. They let me talk, and when I was done, they were happy to issue me another three-year denial. You know what, strangely enough, on leaving the hearing I did not feel bad at all. I was frustrated, and I needed to get things off my chest. I did not curse. I did not raise my voice. I very calmly said what was on my mind. Right or wrong, who is to say? I expected nothing, and I got nothing.

Shortly after this, I was moved to A-Yard. I became part of a community of lifers, of brothers, who had embraced a spirit of change, of positivity, of determination to make lemonade out of lemons. The objective:

to become suitable for parole and return to our loved ones, if they were still around, to make amends. They included all races, nationalities, and creeds: Whites, Blacks, Hispanics, Asians, Catholics, Protestants, Jehovah's Witnesses, Jews, 7th Day Adventists, Muslims, former gangbangers, illegal aliens, Veterans, bikers. My gratitude goes to this hodgepodge of men who had grown tired of living like animals and had decided each in his own way to go in search of and reclaim his humanity. They picked me up and would not let me fold. We played sports together, we had spreads, we talked, we listened. With compassionate honesty we worked on each other's errors in thinking. There was no room for playing victim. We accepted and embraced our present reality. Within this group were men who had been found suitable for parole a number of times only to have the Governor take their dates. Their cases were political hot potatoes that made them candidates for death in prison by old age.

I met a lady psychologist who had taken an interest in working with Veterans at the Colony. The guys from the evening group were asked to participate in this new day group. The old timers resisted. The word "psychologist" spooked them. They thought meeting with her would result in all sorts of negative stuff being added to their files. I decided to meet her and find out for myself.

The lady, a petite Indian woman with a strong will, worked out of the West LA VA. I sat, listened, and observed. She scheduled me for a one-on-one meeting. We talked. She learned about my situation and spoke to me about resilience. In the course of meetings, she encouraged me and the group to observe traditional holidays such as Memorial Day and Veterans Day by reading essays that related to that subject. She filled me with hope. She eventually was responsible for finding me a place to go to if paroled. She introduced me to the works of Viktor Frankl, who wrote: "Everything can be taken from a man but one thing: the last of the human freedoms—to choose one's attitude in any given set of circumstances, to choose one's own way." I totally got that!

As before, I did not have to wait three years. I was summoned back to the Board in November 2016. Like in 2013, I was found suitable for parole again. And once again it would be up to the Governor if I actually left on parole or not. This time I kept my property and payed no attention to well-wishers. I kept my emotions in check and did not allow myself to think of the possibilities. Yet, as the fourth month came into play the pressure started to mount. Group classes at LTOP were a weekly thing. It became fashionable for fellows to get calls from counselors to drop by the office to sign their parole papers. That was a clear indication that you were on your way. No bull. And so, if you were close to D-Day and sitting in class, every time the phone rang your attention would drift. It was a race between getting a pass to go pick up legal mail at the office, which was bad, or hearing the phone ring and being sent to the office to sign papers, which was good. And then it happened. Like winning the lottery. The phone rang, and my name was called.

"Agrio, go see your counselor to sign your parole papers."

Yep. I cried. Right there in front of all those convicts. I didn't care what anyone said or thought. But it was all good. The support was enormous. I felt the love.

The days leading up to my release were highly stressful. I didn't want to leave the cell. I worried that something crazy would go down and I'd be caught up in it, screwing everything up. But guys wanted to kick it, walk the yard one more time. It was hard to say no. So many of them had been there for me when things went wrong. I'd been a part of so many self-help groups. As much as I wanted to avoid it, it was only right I go out and offer hope.

I felt blessed. Well-wishers were everywhere. At work, at chow, walking the yard—lots of handshakes, a few hugs. Even a few guards came by to give me the old "don't come back" speech. I packed a bag with important papers, photos, and a couple hygiene products. The rest I gave away—food, TV, books, clothing, court decisions regarding parole, litigation templates, and more. I was given quite a few phone numbers and addresses. But life is such that trying to keep your head above water prevents you from reaching out to all. I remember talking about those who'd gone before me and wondering why they didn't stay in touch. I found out why. It's like driving fast on the freeway and keeping your eyes on the road or risk getting into a wreck.

The night before was the worst. When the guard threw the bar and got ready for count it was just me and my thoughts. The cell was bare. There were no books to read and no TV to watch. I laid on the bunk and closed my eyes, but sleep wouldn't come. My mind started playing tricks on me. I feared parole would be stopped at the last minute for some bogus reason or another. I'd heard stories of guys getting to R&R only to be told that they'd not received the final okay from Sacramento. A true nightmare. I got up and started pacing. I stood by the window, but the sight of the chain-linked fence adorned with concertina wire was depressing. I kept looking at my watch every two minutes. Time was standing still. I tried to distract myself with positive thoughts. My anxiety only grew.

I got back on the bunk and waited. The plan was for the guard to let me out of my cell at 0530 hours so I could head to R&R for processing. I was dressed and standing by the door at 0400 hours. When 0530 came and nothing happened, I didn't know what to think. Part of me wanted to start banging on the door to get the guard's attention. But that would've been out of character and serve only to piss the guard off. I craned my neck to see if I could spot any early workers and get their attention. Nothing. I sat on the toilet for the umpteenth time even though there was nothing more to unload. I kept reminding myself to stay calm. R&R knew where I was, and if I was running late, they would call the building looking for me.

My tier was second in the rotation for breakfast that day. When we were released, I grabbed my brown bag and jetted out. As I walked past the podium, the guard winked at me and with a smile told me they wanted me at R&R. I couldn't help but think, *Was that fucker messing with my head?* I just kept going. I was in a hurry. Someone asked if I was going to breakfast. Behind me I heard a voice say, "Fuck breakfast! That man is going home."

I got to the gate, and luckily the plaza guard was on the ball and let me through right away. It was smooth sailing to the R&R corridor. I found of couple other parolees waiting, so I relaxed. I was not late. A few minutes later the officer came out with a list in hand and checked to make sure he had the right inmates. I started to feel much better after the paperwork was sorted out and we were told to shed the prison blues. I put on a grey sweat suit I'd saved for the occasion and was ready to go. In the movies guys always leave in a nice suit. Not in real life. There was still one more visit to a holding tank. Transportation was going to wait until minutes before the bus out of San Luis Obispo was ready to leave to walk us out.

When we finally stepped out, it was surreal. Two of us were heading in the same direction so, initially at least, we had each other to help keep it together. The $200 gate money was cut in half with the cost of the ticket. We found out we had to go to Hanford first, then Bakersfield, and then Los Angeles for me. Hanford to Bakersfield was by train. At Bakersfield, my parole buddy and I split up. We hugged each other, wished all the best, and ran to our respective departure spots. The bus left on time, destination Union Station Los Angeles. My head stayed on a swivel, my stomach full of butterflies.

When I walked out of prison April 2017, it was a culture shock. I couldn't even figure out how to get my soda from the machine at Burger King in Hanford. On the train, I kept tripping off people messing with their laptops. And everyone had a phone and paid attention to nothing else. When I arrived in Los Angeles I needed to make a call for a ride to my final destination at the West LA VA. I couldn't find a pay phone anywhere and started to feel panicky. In prison guys were always talking about what's the first thing you were going to do when you got out. Well, it never occurred to me it would be buying a phone.

I found a pay phone a couple of blocks away from the bus terminal at a gas station. I picked up the receiver and dialed zero. A recorded message said I needed to put coins in. I tried to get the gas station attendant to change a twenty for me. He said he could not open the register to give me change. Desperate, I told him about my predicament—I was fresh out of the pen and needed to call a friend for a ride. The look on his face told me he thought I was giving him a line of shit. However, he reached into his pocket and gave me whatever change he found.

Back at the phone I couldn't find Coach's number. I called my mom, who then had to call Coach and tell him where I was. Coach had agreed to pick me up but after he got off work. I waited for about an hour as evening started to roll in. I had no idea if my mom had connected with Coach, but I knew she wouldn't stop trying. I figured the gas station was an easy enough place to find. I figured right.

Coach found me just as I was about to reach out to one of the motorists buying gas for assistance. I'd met Coach at the Colony my first go-round and reconnected with him on my return as he was paroling. A tall Mexican-American fellow, he'd been a baseball player in his young days. He was also a man of his word. Before paroling, he promised to stay in touch with those he left behind, and he did. I was grateful for that.

Before we got in his car, he gave me a bag with shoes and clothing. He then told me I was in good hands because he knew exactly where I needed to go. I wanted to get there right away, afraid I would get in trouble if I was late. Coach kept telling me to relax, that there were no more guards and no more "count time." But I remained anxious as he proceeded to give me the grand tour and drop by the homes of other recently paroled lifers. He took me to eat at Denny's where I ordered steak and dessert. He then took out his phone, took a picture of me eating my first meal as a free man, and sent it to my mom.

We drove up to the *Haven* at West Los Angeles VA just before midnight. My bed was waiting for me, and I was checked in. Word got around quickly enough, and other vets from the prison group came to see me. One fellow let me use an extra phone he had. Another gave me pocket money, and so it went.

While the last execution in California was in 2006, incarcerated people die in California prisons regularly. The most common cause of death in prison is "natural causes" (old age, chronic illness, or disease) followed by homicide at the hands of a law enforcement officer and then suicide. There were 9,909 deaths in CDCR between 2005 and 2018. Law enforcement was responsible for 1,423 of those.

Add to that the fact that in March of 2006 a federal judge placed the entire CDCR healthcare system under receivership after finding the system violated the 8th Amendment to the United Sates Constitution. This unprecedented move came as a result of evidence showing that the state-run healthcare system killed one prisoner every six to seven days. The receiver was granted power to hire, fire, and discipline staff; to make and break contracts; to write and discard policies; and to control every healthcare dollar spent for CDCR's 160,000 prisoners. If a state law, regulation, or contract, including labor agreements [read: the powerful prison guards union (CCPOA)], blocked his way, the receiver would simply ask the judge to waive it. CDCR's only remaining healthcare function was to fund the checks the receiver wrote. The receiver was even told he could build new medical facilities and charge it to California's treasury.

In 2003, CDCR had been ordered to phase in major improvements in its 33 prisons on a court-approved four-year schedule. Detailed in a 1,000-page Policies and Procedures Manual, the plan covered specified needs for Reception Centers, sick call, specialty clinics/consultations, Urgent/Emergency response, infirmary care, preventative care, chronic care, diagnostic services, medication, medical diets, transfers and quality monitoring (QMAT). Later, protocols were added for TB, HIV, and HCV (hepatitis) treatment.

But this massive plan proved more than CDCR could deliver on. When the first phase of implementations was done, a federal judge inspected San Quentin. He was horrified and angry with what he saw. His observations noted a dentist, without washing his hands, using the same glove when moving from one patient's mouth to the next. Clinical treatment rooms had no running water where staff could wash up between patients. Hospital rooms were dank and filthy. Sewage water leaked from one floor to the next. Many hundreds of Reception Center technical parole violators were housed on the floors of the cell blocks, only 12" apart. [This had been a deliberate overpopulation gimmick (bed-vacancy-driven recidivism) to drive guard overtime to $1 million per month at San Quentin.] The judge ordered then-CDCR Director Jeanne Woodford to eliminate those unfit beds immediately.

When I left CDCR in 2017, its healthcare system was still under the supervision of a receiver.

Average time served for released lifers with murder convictions was 12.3 years between 1984 and 2001. By 2013, it was 24.3 years. It currently stands at right around 30 years. The passage of Proposition 89 in 1988 allowed governors to overturn the parole board's parole grants for lifers convicted of murder and to demand additional review for others, a secondary review process used by only four other states. More recently, Marsy's Law of 2008 (Proposition 9) increased possible wait times between parole hearings from 1–5 years to 3–15 years. In 2016, the 9th U.S. Circuit Court of Appeals reversed a district court ruling, finding that Propositions 9 and 89 violated the Ex Post Facto Clause of the U.S. Constitution, which prohibits retroactively increasing prison sentences. Throughout this period, some incarcerated individuals had successfully challenged parole denials by filing writs of habeas corpus. In 2011, the United States Supreme Court limited the federal courts' ability to provide this relief.

The Sentencing Project, a research and advocacy for reform group, found that the release estimates given above are based on the population that is released from prison. They understate the increased punitiveness of the state by omitting the large number of people who died in prison before being paroled. That report also noted that "most lifers will die in prison before they get out on parole," and state records reveal that more lifers with murder convictions died in prison than were paroled between 2000 and 2011.

I'd narrowly avoided becoming part of this gruesome statistic.

18

My new home was actually a drug and alcohol recovery program run by the Salvation Army. I was placed in a room with three other vets. Two of them were under heavy medication and slept all day and all night. They left the bed only for meals. This was another institution but of a different color. There was even a security guard at the entrance, which had me thinking I couldn't leave the building without permission. It took me weeks before I got comfortable with the idea that no one was paying attention to what I was doing.

I drove up a Friday night and had to see my parole officer in Van Nuys first thing Monday morning. Various Joes, including my old Sergeant-at-Arms Russell, tried to explain to me all the different buses I'd have to take to get there. I feared I'd get lost. I didn't resolve the issue until late Sunday evening when I convinced one of the residents to take me there in exchange for a small fee. The money was well spent. I would've never made it there on my own. I saw my parole officer and was given my marching orders.

Russell, my old Jewish mate and a guy who was good at making himself useful, had managed to take control of the Haven's kitchen. He immediately brought me into the fold and put me to work as a volunteer serving food. He took time to share with me what he'd learned during the time he was out. I learned from him that I didn't have time to waste in finding another place. The Salvation Army was being evicted from VA property and their program essentially shut down. The program had been in place since 1994 and provided transitional housing and meals to veterans based on "Grant Per Diem," granted by the VA. But effective September 30, 2017, their enhanced-use lease with West Los Angeles VA was being terminated because of "performance issues." All the programs they offered and the 200 beds available to homeless vets would be gone. I was homeless and on the verge of becoming even more homeless in just a few months.

I took advantage of the time I had to secure proper identification and renew my driver's license. At the first opportunity I caught a bus to Santa Monica, walked to the beach, put on a pair of shorts, and got in the water. The water was cold, but I didn't care. I let the waves bang me around and knock me off balance. I looked up to the heavens and thanked the Lord for bringing me this far in spite of everything. Tears mixed in with salt water and for a brief moment it felt like I was that boy at the beach back in Panama when the road was still straight and smooth. I let out a primal scream and repeated the word "freedom" over and over as people on the beach wondered if I'd escaped from Atascadero State Hospital.

From the Haven I moved to the DOM, another drug program, this one run by the VA just a couple of buildings away. This was a rehab program that lasted three months. During intake I was told not to get comfortable and find another place to go in a hurry or risk ending up on the streets. From there I went to US Vets in Inglewood. This place was more like prison. I was put in a small cell (they called it a room with two bunk beds) with three other inmates and had to account for my every move. There was a curfew. All the old feelings and emotions I had while in prison started to come back again.

During group therapy with lifer vets I learned about Hope Harbor, a Salvation Army shelter in downtown Los Angeles near USC. I'd had a good experience working with Salvation Army before so asked the group coordinator to make arrangements for me. Hope Harbor gave me a room with a key and a year to find permanent residency. The staff was kind and decent to me, but bed bugs and having to surrender my medications to them, to be dispensed only at certain times, made me feel like I was still in a bad dream.

With the help of HUD-VASH I finally got my own apartment. But that program is no piece of cake either. They help as long as you remain in the gutter. If you show progress and a desire towards independence, meaning you get a job, they cut you off or reduce assistance without ensuring you are good for the long run. They are supposed to help with rent by paying two-thirds of it, and they do if your only income is through other government programs. If you start making money, the percentage is adjusted. Proof is necessary via a mountain of paperwork, and a case manager is assigned to shadow you with more diligence than a parole officer. You never feel like you can breathe easy. Maybe there is a reason for them being that way. I don't know the history. But I think when it comes to vets the bottom line should be they pay the two-thirds for a minimum of two years regardless of the nature of your income. This would allow vets to find a decent place to live other than a rat-infested room in the vicinity of skid row. Property owners in decent neighborhoods don't want to be associated with Section 8 and HUD. I guess it's bad for their image and the reputation of their hood.

It was while at the DOM that I was diagnosed with PTSD and Tinnitus. These conditions dated back to my military service. I had been living with these issues all this time not knowing that help was available. When I left the service the term PTSD was not part of the mental health vocabulary and the symptoms were mostly associated with combat vets.

I'm so glad that's not the case today. My PTSD was probably exacerbated by my work as a police officer.

Today, I would like to think that I'm free, but not really. There is a tight leash attached to my neck. It bothers me that I cannot vote and thus participate in the political process during these extraordinary times in our country. I think Assembly Bill AB2466 should be amended to allow parolees to vote, especially after a protracted term of incarceration. Parolees are among the best-informed citizens in the country and are not easily buffaloed with dumb Propositions like the Three Strikes Law. And who better understands the need for change than those who've had to deal with the consequences of living in the mud. It bothers me that I cannot travel to visit my family overseas, pandemic or not. It bothers me that I won't get an opportunity to put my law degree to work.

I read somewhere about Kanye West calling for the abolishment of the 13th Amendment. As you may know, the 13th Amendment to the United States Constitution abolished slavery and involuntary servitude, except as punishment for a crime. In Congress, it was passed by the Senate on April 8, 1864, and by the House on January 31, 1865. The amendment was ratified by the required number of states on December 6, 1865.

While I don't personally believe it should be abolished, I certainly believe it should be amended to remove the words "except as punishment for a crime." Allowing prisoners to be viewed as slaves frees politicians and gatekeepers to treat inmates as disposable garbage, or better said "3/5 persons," not human beings. This is especially so since the media is not allowed inside prisons to talk to prisoners and gauge conditions as they exist in real time, only as part of some dog and pony show carefully choreographed. Furthermore, having the amendment serves as a reminder of the root cause of the division and mistrust that exists in the country today and provides a legal basis for preventing any repeat of history. Slavery should not be condoned in any area of American society. Period.

I'm still trying to put my life back together. I anticipated struggles and setbacks. I didn't think adjusting to life in LA would be easy. However, adding a pandemic—COVID19—to the mix and watching calls for social justice take center stage all over and simultaneously have produced an odd mixture of death and survival. A World War Z.

EPILOGUE

"I grasped the meaning of the greatest secret that human poetry and human thought and belief have to impart: The salvation of man is through love and in love."

Viktor Frankl

This is by no means a great work of literature, but it's a story I needed to tell. It is the sad tale of an immigrant. People love to talk about America, the land of opportunities, as if every immigrant that comes here finds instant happiness and success. Well, the ugly truth is that although opportunities do exist few make it big. The vast majority find themselves overcoming one hardship after another. Racism, greed, avarice, jealousy, envy, hate, prejudice, deceit, duplicity, et cetera are in your shadow, disturbing your sleep.

You're never really sure where you belong or who you can trust. This isn't really a problem when things are going well, but when things go bad that's when the truth you've been ignoring and avoiding catches up with you—you're alone, in a country that doesn't recognize you as its own, no native culture, no community, no resources other than the ones you can afford to buy, surrounded by strangers who are eager to strip you of whatever little you had and leave you for vultures to fill their bellies.

Battered and bruised you ask yourself the questions: *Where did I come from? Where am I going? Why am I here? Was this my destiny? Could it have been different?*

I did almost 30 years of prison time in various state penitentiaries. The first time I heard the term "abuser" applied to me was at trial. I scoffed at the thought. Surely they had it wrong. I was a man who'd tried to do the right thing by a woman who didn't appreciate it. That was my thinking. Nevertheless, deep down inside I felt guilty and knew punishment was inevitable.

What I wasn't prepared for was the kind of punishment I would receive. And here I must point out that I'm referring to "man's punishment." There is a spiritual component to this that hopefully will end with death. No matter what people say about this, it's just hard to forgive yourself after unnecessarily taking someone's life and to continue pursuing happiness like everyone else. If you have a conscience, your conscience will bother you for the rest of your life.

But back to man's punishment. Since I fully cooperated with the authorities, made all my court appearances while on bail and the eventual findings of the jury, I thought I would end up doing twelve, maybe fifteen years of prison time. Instead, I ended up doing almost thirty years.

There were times when I felt I'd never get out. Being a model prisoner meant nothing, and legal challenges to flawed decisions only brought more wrath upon me. Officials did nothing to help me change as a man. That was ultimately my responsibility. They sought instead to destroy me physically and emotionally as a form of revenge. I don't know if this was related to the nature of my crime or the fact that I'd been in law enforcement and my wife was on her way to working in law enforcement. Who knows? Maybe it was just politics. The truth is that every "lifer" I know has a horror story to tell.

And while the system was methodically going about quietly killing me, no one in the community was being deterred from committing acts of domestic violence. Upon my release I returned to the world to discover that abuse was and still is prevalent in our society and no one really understands what causes this and what to do to fix it. About the best the general consensus has come up with is that if you find yourself in an abusive relationship you must run and try to get away from it as quickly as you can. This advice fails to consider all the factors that make relationships complicated. And while asking for help is no doubt a good thing, a cure for the disease, so to speak, still eludes us as a race. Some of the brightest and most intelligent and accomplished human beings have had a go at this and they haven't come close to solving the puzzle. So, we continue to spend our resources on punishing individuals while failing to get to the root cause of the problem.

I wish I could say that this book provides the answer, but sadly that's not the case. My wish is that those who read my account can recognize in themselves the pattern of behavior that can bring about dire consequences and do something about the situation in an adult, responsible way rather than ignoring the obvious. Each individual looking at themselves in the mirror and deciding to change can make a huge difference. So can putting a stop to glorifying violence in the media. I don't know how we make heroes of violent men in one instance and then condemn the same behavior in another. As humans we have proven incapable of recognizing the difference.

Only a handful of people that knew me from prior to my incarceration still remain in touch with me. My mother and my brother are two of them. Everyone else in my life today is a new acquaintance. Most of these new acquaintances are professionals keeping an eye on me to make sure

I stay on the straight and narrow. The others are old men like me whom I met while doing time and who experienced their own hell and are now living a life full of gratitude.

There are many people to thank for the care and compassion they showed in helping me to understand the errors of my ways. I wish I could name them all or reach out and thank them personally, but rules being what they are, I can't. However, I remain eternally grateful that they were placed in my path like angels sent by God. I find it ironic that the vast majority of these angels were women. Go figure.

I have come to believe that the unpredictability of abuse and domestic violence make it so that the first physical attack should lead to drastic measures. Men should seek immediate professional help, and women should abandon the relationship if their men refuse to do so. To believe things can be remedied without help or that the promises made in the aftermath of an incident are sustainable is the equivalent of playing Russian roulette. On any given day, things can get out of hand and tragedy can literally destroy the lives of many.

Self-forgiveness has proven a difficult concept for me to grasp much less apply to my life. When I was young, I didn't entertain the thought of forgiveness very much at all. I lived in the moment, dreaming about what wonders adulthood would bring. If I used the word from time to time, it was probably to get out of some predicament. This, in spite of the fact that as a Catholic attending Catholic school, I was constantly repeating the word in the Lord's Prayer, but in those moments it had an empty meaning.

I say the Lord's Prayer now as an adult having lived through the consequences of my mistakes and still have trouble with the meaning of "forgiveness" but for different reasons. In the prayer, we ask God to forgive us our trespasses. Allowing for this feeling of forgiveness for my past wrongdoings often seems like an impossible task, especially in regards to forgiving myself. At times I feel I struggle with the concept of self-forgiveness because I don't know what it looks like or what it should feel like. Other times, I worry about the possible negative effects forgiveness of myself might have on my life.

I have been accused of lacking empathy for others, and I worry what the effect of self-forgiveness would have on that. Would I be giving myself too much slack? How would those who know my story feel about that? What judgment would I subject myself to? I also worry about losing my motivation to embrace living amends as a worthy goal. Those of you who are familiar with the 12 step programs such as AA and NA will recognize this term. Living amends means living a completely new lifestyle and being committed to that lifestyle (in part for those I harmed and in part for myself). Living amends means making genuine changes, that my behavior and actions be true and honest and follow an emotionally sober path. This is important to me because I don't want to repeat the mistakes of the past.

As hard as I try not to beat myself up for the wrongs committed, my soul and my spirit remain restless. I pray for divine guidance to obtain peace of mind. But up until now that peace of mind escapes me.

I've read and listened to the opinions of others on the subject. For instance, *Radical Self-Forgiveness* by Colin Tipping and Nataly Kogan's program Sounds True on "Self-Compassion." I understand the importance of achieving or embracing self-forgiveness. I take the suggestions to heart. However, the truth is: I don't feel any changes in my consciousness that indicate I've moved forward. This is troublesome to me. It opens the door to depression and other unhealthy thoughts and feelings.

Often times, I feel as if those whom I've wronged would indicate clearly that they forgave me, then that would pave the way for me to feel it's okay to move on. There is definitely a connection there, even though I've no reason to believe that this will happen. The end result is that I feel I'm waiting for something to happen, I'm not sure what, that would make it okay for me to stop beating myself up. I suspect the feeling is linked to not having a relationship with my son and my former in-laws.

Living like this is hard. Joy, love, happiness, excitement, and the like are on hold, waiting for this issue to be resolved. And when something happens that brings me face to face with the consequences of my bad decisions, the clouds of shame, guilt, regret, and disgust knock on my door to remind me they are still around. I pray, meditate, and I attend individual therapy to regain my focus and find emotional balance. Some days are better than others, as they say.

In the second part of the Lord's Prayer, we are asked to forgive others for their wrongdoing. I've taken to heart what is meant by this as a result of my pain. I can say, with some degree of certainty, that because of what I went through, today I've a better perspective of what causes misery and suffering in the world, in myself and others. I'm more vulnerable and connected to those around, whether relatives, friends, acquaintances, or strangers. I guess you could say I've become more accepting and less judgmental.

If I had to imagine what forgiveness or self-forgiveness would feel like, I've a vision of nature and its splendor, with birds singing and a cool breeze caressing my face, sunshine, and my heart at peace with creation and its creator. Whether I experience that in this life I cannot say, but my faith is strong and I trust God will make me an instrument of his will and make it so my experiences will help others feel they are not alone.

When you love someone, you don't do harm to them, physically or emotionally. You want what is best for them and try to be supportive. Couples will invariably disagree on a variety of things, but when there is care and compassion, you talk things out in a calm and rational manner. I personally believe that a relationship that is swimming in the pool of resentment, bitterness, jealousy, mistrust, and anger is best severed sooner rather than later for the sake of all involved. I also believe that if you want a relationship with a woman, it is best to get to know her first before you have sex. If all you want is sex, then have sex and move on and be sure to use protection to avoid unwanted complications. If you take time to get to know a woman and you cannot accept her as she is, chances are that relationship won't work for you. If you believe you have the power or ability to shape someone into what you'd like them to be, you are setting yourself up for abusive behavior and domestic violence.

If you're interested in starting a relationship with someone, it's a good idea to explore what it is you're looking for; what you bring to the table and how much you know about who you really are. Failure to answer these questions will have you living dazed and confused and on the edge of a precipice.

Famous people continue to make headlines with domestic violence. Denials are quick to follow as are attempts to point fingers and assess blame. Unless someone died, the episodes are treated the same as if one were arrested for drunk driving. Lawyers are brought in, and deals are cut to ensure minimum punishment. Judges enjoy ordering men to attend a year of domestic violence classes. But having sat in those classes myself I can testify that very few participants see this as an opportunity to address a serious problem. Their only concern is to receive credit for attendance so they can report back to the judge that they complied with the order.

Many feel that they were provoked into becoming violent by their mates, that they had no choice or that they were only defending themselves. And underneath it all is a strong belief in male privilege. A belief they refuse to give up.

Children and substance abuse complicate matters even more. If there are issues with drugs or alcohol, those issues have to be dealt with before trying to tackle abuse or domestic violence. And interfering with parental rights only fuels more resentment. The system tries, but it seldom gets it right.

In the end, participants continue troubled relationships wishing only to be left to their own devices. That is, until there's a need for the law to get involved.

As you have read, it took me a long time before I even began to accept the fact that I'd been an abusive husband. That I spent so much time in prison helped because I had plenty of hours to contemplate and look inward. *And I'd reached a point where I was willing to examine my true nature.* That's not to say it takes thirty years to get there. But you have to reach that point.

Outside of prison, day-to-day activities make it difficult for at-risk individuals to embark on the kind of honest self-examination that brings about change in attitude and beliefs.

Further complicating matters is the fact that abuse and domestic violence come in a variety of shapes and designs. There are men who are flat-out sick and abusive and enjoy tormenting their mates daily. They live to terrorize and exert power and control over their spouses or girlfriends. That is the extreme.

On the other hand, there are men who have no history of abusive behavior, but circumstances are such that in the heat of an argument they lose control of their emotions and end up committing battery. The law makes no distinction between the extremes. Whether it's an isolated incident of domestic violence, or a history of abusive behavior, all labels and dispositions are the same. And even if no one dies, the consequences will be felt for a long time. Careers and livelihoods destroyed.

Alcoholics and substance abusers have AA and NA to support them in their recovery efforts. Men in complicated relationships need something similar to address their issues and explore non-violent alternatives without the weight of the law on their necks. I believe that there is more willingness to learn and explore when it's done voluntarily rather than when one is forced to do it.

Before I leave you, let me share with you some good news. I have re-married and I believe this time it's for good. I have so many more tools in my tool-box I'm confident of that. But if for some reason we cannot make it to the end of the rainbow, it's okay. I will never stop in my pursuit of happiness.

I pray my story helps all who read it make better decisions in their lives.

Remember:

No matter what—violence is not an option.

ACKNOWLEDGEMENTS

Let me first say thank you to everyone at Book Baby who has in some way cared for this book.

Thank you to the UCLA Wordcommandos for their support and encouragement in writing this memoir, especially to Robert Morgan Fisher "Gunny," for his love and support.

Thank you to all the good people at the CMC LTOP program and the various mental health professionals there who provided individual therapy for all the hours they spent re-educating me.

Thank you to the psychologists at the West LA VA who finally diagnosed my PTSD condition and today continue to provide care and support, especially Doctors Anjali Alimchandani, Shoba Sreenivasan, and Steven Ganzell. Also, LCSW's Lyndon Olmeda, Caryn Shein, and Rima Simon.

Thank you to Chrysalis – Santa Monica for helping me ease back into the work force and assisting with furniture, linen, and home appliances as I moved from transitional housing into my own apartment.

And, of course, I am grateful to my mom Juana, my brother Frank, and my wife Marina for all the love and support.

To everyone whose books I've read over the years, whose sentences were helping me to make sentences, to think, to articulate: gratitude.

And finally, Dear Reader, as always, *as always*, I am grateful to you. Here is wishing that your journey be less complicated than mine after sharing in my experience.